ISBN: 9781313691314

Published by:
HardPress Publishing
8345 NW 66TH ST #2561
MIAMI FL 33166-2626

Email: info@hardpress.net
Web: http://www.hardpress.net

FEB 19 1914

NOV 5
NOV 19 1923

Ti mando i pensieri e

WORKS BY G. CAMPBELL MORGAN

A New Popular Edition
THE CRISES OF THE CHRIST.
Dr. Morgan's Most Comprehensive Work. 8vo, cloth, $1.50 net.

A FIRST CENTURY MESSAGE TO TWENTIETH CENTURY CHRISTIANS.
Addresses upon "The Seven Churches of Asia." Cloth, net $1.00.

THE SPIRIT OF GOD.
12mo, cloth, $1.25.

GOD'S METHODS WITH MAN.
In Time—Past, Present and Future. With colored chart. 12mo, paper, 50 cents. Cloth, $1.00.

WHEREIN HAVE WE ROBBED GOD?
Malachi's Message to the Men of To-Day. 12mo, cloth, 75 cents.

GOD'S PERFECT WILL.
16mo, cloth, 50 cents net.

LIFE PROBLEMS.
Little Books Series. Long 16mo, 50 cents.

THE TEN COMMANDMENTS.
Studies in the Law of Moses and the Law of Christ. 12mo, cloth, 50 cents net.

DISCIPLESHIP.
Little Books Series. Long 16mo, cloth, 50c.

THE HIDDEN YEARS AT NAZARETH.
Quiet Hour Series. 18mo, cloth, 25 cents.

THE TRUE ESTIMATE OF LIFE.
An Entirely New, Revised and Enlarged Edition. 80 cents net.

"ALL THINGS NEW."
A Message to New Converts. 16mo, paper, 10 cents net.

THE LIFE

OF THE

CHRISTIAN

BY

REV. G. CAMPBELL MORGAN, D. D.

Chicago : New York : Toronto
Fleming H. Revell Company
London and Edinburgh
1904.

COPYRIGHT 1904
BY
REV. G. CAMPBELL MORGAN, D. D.

Dedicated to

my friend, Albert Swift

CONTENTS

THE LIFE OF THE CHRISTIAN:—

I	ITS NATURE	7
II	ITS SUSTENANCE	27
III	ITS EXPRESSION	45
IV	ITS CONSCIOUSNESS	63
V	ITS TESTING	81
VI	ITS VALUE	97

THE MASTER'S HAND.

Phil. i. 21.

"To me to live is Christ," and yet the days
    Are days of toiling men;
We rise at morn, and tread the beaten ways,
    And lay us down again.

How is it that this base, unsightly life
    Can yet be Christ alone?
Our common need, and weariness, and strife,
    While common days wear on?

Then saw I how before a Master wise
    A shapeless stone was set;
He said, 'Therein a form of beauty lies
    Though none behold it yet.'

'When all beside it shall be hewn away,
    That glorious shape shall stand,
In beauty of the everlasting day,
    Of the unsullied land.'

Thus is it with the homely life around,
    There hidden, Christ abides;
Still by the single eye for ever found
    That seeketh none beside.

When hewn and shaped till self no more is found,
    Self, ended at Thy Cross;
The precious freed from all the vile around,
    No gain, but blessed loss.

Then Christ alone remains—the former things
    Forever passed away;
And unto Him the heart in gladness sings
    All through the weary day.
              —H. Suso.
    "Hymns of Ter Steegen, Suso and Others."

THE LIFE OF THE CHRISTIAN—ITS NATURE.

"Thy nature, gracious Lord impart!
  Come quickly from above
Write Thy new name upon my heart
  Thy new, best name of love."
                              —Wesley.

"Every fragment of moral beauty in a regenerated life is a mirroring of a little fragment, at least, of the image of God on which our eyes may gaze. Every true Christian life is in an imperfect degree, and yet truly, a new incarnation; 'Christ liveth in me.'"—J. R. Miller.

"For Thou to me art all in all,
  My honour and my wealth,
My heart's desire, my body's strength,
  My soul's eternal health.

* * * * * *

O Jesus! Jesus! sweetest Lord!
  What art Thou not to me?
Each hour brings joy before unknown,
  Each day new liberty!

What limit is there to thee, love?
  Thy flight where wilt thou stay?
On! on! our Lord is sweeter far
  Today than yesterday.

Oh love of Jesus! Blessed love!
  So will it ever be;
Time cannot hold thy wondrous growth,
  No, nor eternity!"
                              —F. W. Faber.

CHAPTER I.

THE LIFE OF THE CHRISTIAN—ITS NATURE.

"And Barnabas went forth to Tarsus to seek for Saul; and when he had found him, he brought him unto Antioch. And it came to pass, that even for a whole year they were gathered together with the church, and taught much people; and that the disciples were called Christians first in Antioch." Acts xi. 25-26.

"And Agrippa said unto Paul, With but little persuasion thou wouldest fain make me a Christian." Acts xxvi. 28.

"But if a man suffer as a Christian, let him not be ashamed; but let him glorify God in this name." I Peter iv. 16.

"The disciples were called Christians first in Antioch." "With but little persuasion thou wouldest fain make me a Christian." "If a man suffer as a Christian, let him not be ashamed; but let him glorify God in this name."

These are the only occasions where the word "Christian" occurs in the New Testament. This word, occurring so rarely, and gradually passing into common use, has become almost commonplace. Yet the word in itself has a deep significance and suggestiveness.

Seeing therefore that with the passing of the centuries the word has now come to be so widely used, it is interesting and valuable to go back to the beginnings, and consider what it meant in the early days.

The name by which the followers of Christ were most generally known at that period was that of disciples.

They also spoke of themselves as believers, as brethren in Christ, as those who were of "the Way." But they did not speak of themselves as Christians. The first time the word Christian is used, it is in the way of description. It has been said that these men of Antioch, proverbially witty and clever, created this as a term of opprobrium, a kind of nickname. I am not at all sure of the correctness of that view. It was certainly a name given to these followers of Christ by those who were without. The disciples did not call themselves Christians. They "were called Christians first in Antioch." The people of Antioch observed these people, took note of them as to their conversation, and their habits, and said, They are Christians. Those not themselves Christians were the first to apply the name to the followers of Christ, and it was intended to describe them.

The next occurrence of the word is where a king used it, in a tone of supercilious contempt. The Revision has altered the text, and corrected a very popular misconception. Agrippa did not for a moment mean to say that Paul very nearly persuaded him to be a Christian. On the contrary, noticing the earnestness of Paul, and the aggressiveness of his spirit, and having listened to his argument, in disdain for him the king said, "With but little persuasion thou wouldest fain make me a Christian."

Only once in the New Testament is the word "Christian" used of Christian people by a Christian. Peter made use of it in his epistle, and yet even here, if the whole context be read, it will be found that in all probability he was quoting from others. Writing of the fact that believers suffer persecution on account of their pure life, he declared that those outside would wonder that they did not run to every "excess of riot," but he added, "if any man suffer as a Christian, let him glorify God in this name;" and thus it is seen that the expression was probably a quotation from the language of those outside. If it was intended that opprobrium should attach to it, then the apostle charged them not to be ashamed of it, but rather to glorify God in it. Let the name be used, and its true significance revealed.

These are the only occurrences in the New Testament, and yet the word has taken hold upon us, and now throughout the world the followers of Christ are spoken of as Christians. Thus the word has come to have a far wider meaning than it had when the men of Antioch used it to describe the disciples, when Agrippa used it in supercilious contempt, or when Peter used it recognizing that it was being made use of as a term of reproach.

If we examine these occasions of New Testament use, we shall find that all the values that attach to the name today are to be found in them in germ.

First let us examine these instances carefully, in order that we may see how it was used at the beginning; and then let us go behind these early uses of the name, and find out what it really meant. Thus I think we shall be able to understand what the nature of the Christian life really is.

The fact that the term was first applied to the disciples by outsiders is in itself suggestive. Why did the men of Antioch call these people Christians? There can be but one answer, a simple answer, and yet including the whole fact. They saw that these people had been with the Christ in spirit, if not in actual personality, and that they had learned of Him. They talked of Christ, lived for

Christ, worked for Christ. They had caught His Spirit, they were occupied with His business, and were manifesting Him in character and conduct; and the men of Antioch said, These people are Christians, men connected with Christ in some way.

For a moment think of the story of the history of Antioch. This was God's new starting point. The church at Jerusalem had failed to obey the law. It had become self-centred, conceited, and self-satisfied, interested only in the movements emanating from its authority. This church was the most dire and dismal failure, never realizing its own privilege and power. Obedience to the Master's plain injunction to begin at Jerusalem and to go to the uttermost part of the earth, was only realized as they were driven out from Jerusalem by persecution. God has always been abandoning an ordained channel in order to take some new one, that His work and purpose may be fulfilled. Barnabas found Saul, brought him to Antioch, and there they spent a whole year teaching the disciples, and it was at this place that the men of Antioch named these people Christians.

The relationship must have been marked and positive. What they were, how they lived, and what was evidently the impulse of their life constrained outsiders to name them Christians. Coming from outsiders, the name is of greater value. The force of this fact may best be felt by asking, how many persons would name us Christians if we did not in so many words declare ourselves to be such.

The supreme fact evident in the lives of these people was that they had to do with Christ, and so the men of Antioch called them Christians. Therefore the name first signified that these people manifested in outward life their relationship to Christ.

Passing to the next occasion of the use of the word, we find ourselves in the presence of a familiar and yet beautiful picture. Paul with the chain of his imprisonment upon him, is arguing his case before Agrippa. It is impossible to read that argument without discovering the fact that Paul was far more anxious to bring Agrippa face to face with his Master, than he was to defend himself as in the presence of Agrippa. I do not say that there is no defence of himself, for it is indeed a most remarkable one, showing Paul's mastery of the law of his people, and his understanding of the technicalities thereof. But surging through all, is the great passion of his heart so to present Christ, and tell the story of his own life, as to compel men into a like loyalty to his beloved Lord, to capture men for Christ. This is what impressed Agrippa. He saw most evidently in the passion of the man as he talked, that his intention was to press him toward the Christ; and at last, looking upon the eloquent and earnest man, he said, "With but little persuasion thou wouldest fain make me a Christian." Agrippa was a remarkable man, learned in all matters of his people, acquainted with the prophets, as Paul indicates, and yet a man whose deeds must be nameless, a depraved dilletante, amusing himself for an odd hour with a notable case at law. But feeling the glow and fervor and enthusiasm of Paul he exclaimed, "With but little persuasion thou wouldest fain make me a Christian." He was astonished, surprised, perhaps startled, but supremely disdainful. In this use of the word we have a further revelation of what a Christian is. He is not only a disciple of Christ, himself loyal to Christ, his own life centering about Christ; but one whose passion and purpose is to bring men to Christ, one who so speaks of Christ as to recommend Him, and to constrain other people toward Him. It would perhaps be difficult to find a more superlative instance. This man Agrippa, with no intention or thought of Christianity as something to be impressed with, having not the slightest leaning toward Christ, simply listening to this prisoner, at last discovers what he is trying to do; and recognizes, all unknowingly, one of the sure signs of a Christian, that of desire to make someone else a Christian too.

We have thus in the second place the thought of propagandism. First, personal discipleship; and then the attempt to constrain some others to discipleship.

Then passing to the last instance we have still another suggestion. Peter's use of the word suggests that a Christian is one who suffers the reproaches attached to Christ. This is the whole argument of the section of the epistle from which the quotation is made. The apostle recognizes that there must be suffering and reproach for the name of Christ. Writing to believers, Peter says to them in effect, You are suffering reproach for the name of Christ. You are living in the midst of impurity the life of the pure; and the quality of your purity is not the quality of merely ethical morality, but the purity of separateness from all the things that are evil. Christians therefore are those who are separated from evil in thought, in desire, in action; and who, because of that separation, will have to suffer reproach.

Thus we find in the use of the word, fundamental truths concerning the nature of the life of the Christian.

First, the Christian is a disciple of Christ, one whose whole life centres in Christ, and whose life circles about Christ, so that it becomes manifested to the world that that person is a follower of Jesus Christ. Secondly, the Christian is one who is not merely himself loyal to Christ, but into whose heart there has entered a great passion of desire to win others for Christ. In the third place, the Christian is one who, because of that devotion and loyalty to Christ, and the separation which it entails from the evil of the age, and the methods and the maxims of men, will suffer reproach for Christ, will be a puzzle to those about him, utterly misunderstood by them; and suffering reproach, will glory in it, rejoice in the midst of it, counting the reproach of Christ as being of more value than all the treasures men hold most dear.

These are but the statements of the outward and evident facts. Behind them lies that which is causative. The profounder question is, What makes a Christian to be such a person as this? It is well sometimes to measure ourselves by the outside vision, but it is not always safe, if that is the only method. Let us consider this deeper fact. What made these people at Antioch such people that even the men of Antioch called them Christians? What made Paul so enthusiastic in the declaration of his message, that even Agrippa felt the constraint upon him toward Christ, even though he sneeringly put it away? What is it that makes people so separate from evil, and so devoted to Christ, that they suffer reproach, and are content to suffer and glory in the same? The answer to these questions is to be found in the declaration of the fact that the secret lying behind all these external manifestations is that of Christ Himself formed in the believer. His living presence constrains to loyalty, creates compassion, and constitutes the cause and comfort of the sufferings.

No person is a Christian simply by contemplating Christ from the outside, and attempting to imitate Him. No study of the Christian fact, and acceptance of it intellectually, will ever be sufficient for the realization of the ideals suggested by the New Testament use of the word. Not by imitation, nor by intellectual assent to all the truths of Christianity does any one become a Christian. If these three ideals are fulfilled it is because Christ Himself, the living, present, eternal Christ has taken possession of the inner life, and from that centre directs, controls, suggests, and thus reveals Himself.

A Christian then, is a revelation of Christ, because the Christ within shines through the whole external life.

There may be many who think of themselves as Christians who are yet far from the fulfillment of this ideal. There is a broad sense in which they are correct. For instance, we speak of Christian nations, and of course there is a sense in which this is a correct description, inasmuch as the dominant religious idea of certain nations is Christian. Yet as to deepest meaning it is a degradation of the word to call any existing nation Christian. If the individual units composing the nation are considered, the larger proportion of people are not even avowedly Christian. And even taking the professing Church, it is very questionable whether a large number can truly be described as Christian. There is no Christian nation save that holy nation, which is at the same time "an elect race, a royal priesthood, . . . a people for God's own possession." It is an awful and terrible truth that the line of demarcation between the Church and the world has been almost obliterated. Many are Christians today because they are not Mohammedans or Hebrews.

A true Christian is one indwelt by, and dominated by Christ, so that Christ is able to reveal Himself through that one. Remembering the great internal force of the indwelling Christ, directing, controlling, suggesting, and thus expressing Himself through His disciples, it becomes evident that when the men of Antioch looked they saw Christ. That man is a Christian, a man of one idea, said they. He thinks of Christ, he speaks of Christ, he sings of Christ, he lives for Christ, he is like Christ, he is manifesting Christ, he is a Christian. Wherever the life is under the control of Christ it is being transformed into the likeness of Christ. We cannot be Christians without Christ manifesting Himself in us. If He shall command us to love our enemies, and if in the power of His indwelling might, we begin to do it, then we immediately manifest Him through such action.

The Master said, "I am the Light of the world," but He also said to His disciples, "Ye are the light of the world." The only way in which a Christian is the light of the world is by the Christ life being his life, and so shining through him. It is not a case of reflection merely. It is the actual outshining of the Christ life within. The men of Antioch named these men Christians, not merely because they were Christ's men and Christ's women in the sense of property, but because being under the immediate government of the indwelling Christ, He was revealed through their life and service.

So also with the second phase of suggestion. Look again at the man standing before the king, wearing his

B

chain, and pleading his cause. What is it makes this man so much in earnest, so persuasive as he tells the story of his own experience? It is impossible to contemplate him without seeing that the indwelling Saviour looks through his eyes, and loves Agrippa through his heart, and longs after him through his desire. Paul's passion to persuade Agrippa is Christ's passion to save him. It was Christ in Paul who argued, and spoke, and constrained, and manifested tenderness. It was under the spell of Christ in Paul that Agrippa passed, when resisting that spell he said, "With but little persuasion thou wouldest fain make me a Christian."

We lack here, even more than in the first respect. We have come to speak of winning souls as the business of evangelists. While I still believe God gives some men special gifts by the Holy Spirit, equipping them for the work of evangelists, every Christian ought to be an evangelist, if the evangel has taken possession of the life. The first business of every Christian is that of drawing others to Jesus Christ, by a great burning passion bringing men into the liberty, the love, the light, the joy, until even Agrippa, the dilettante, and debased, feels the drawing toward Christ.

And yet once more. Why is it that men suffer reproach for Christ? It is the reproach of Christ that they suffer. Do not minimize that statement. It is not merely reproach *for* Christ, it is the reproach *of* Christ. That very separation from evil which stirred enmity in the heart of men against Christ is the condition of life which creates reproach for the believer. The purity which contradicts impurity, the light which reveals darkness, the separateness to God which is a perpetual rebuke to rebellion against God; this, which in the life of Jesus issued in the Cross, being reproduced in the life of the believer, is the occasion of reproach and suffering. There is a morality today that makes its boast, and claims to stand side by side with Christianity, yet which is no more akin to the purity of Jesus Christ than the feeble rushlight is to the sunlight. There is a morality which is merely morality conditioned by the existence of the policeman, but it cannot be compared with the purity of Jesus Christ. His was the purity of eternal life, spiritual consciousness. His was not the purity which drew Him away from men. It was a purity so positive, and high, and spiritual, a purity that consisted of such intimate intercourse with God and heaven and eternity, that He could talk to publicans and sinners and harlots, and maintain His uprightness and integrity and reputation; even when a few cynical and critical Pharisees, whose whole idea of righteousness was that which consisted in externality, said of Him, "This Man receiveth sinners, and eateth with them," by which they meant to say, If He touches pitch, He will be contaminated. Yet the general concensus of opinion is that He stands alone in His purity, a purity separate from evil, that enabled Him to touch all the common places of life.

These men to whom Peter wrote were living in that realm of purity, measuring everything by the standards of eternity, bringing all the details of life into the light of the infinite, until there breathed through their every day living the very genius of spiritual and eternal verities. And no one can begin to live like that without suffering reproach. When there comes into the life the aloofness that sets men away from the world, enabling them to touch it only to deliver it, then they will be marked off as Puritanical, a little peculiar. The age of persecution has not passed, though the external manifestations of persecution may be different.

So through all these illustrations this is seen, that the Christian is one in whom Christ dwells, and through whom Christ lives and works and speaks. The indwelling Christ compels the loyalty of life and will, and a Christian is such because his whole life circles around the indwelling Christ, and his whole heart is filled with Christ's compassion, and his whole life is poured forth in sacrificial service.

A Christian is a Christ one. That may not be correct from the standard of etymology, and yet it is the true meaning of the word. A Christ one is one in whom Christ, the spiritual and the eternal, repeats the human life which He lived and manifested in the world. With Christ as the indwelling Lord, the Christian is a disciple. With Christ as the indwelling compassion, the Christian is a worker. With Christ as the indwelling purity, the Christian must bear His reproach, and yet glory in it as the highest honour.

To sum up. The nature of the Christian life is Christ's life taking hold upon all the inner life of man, changing, dominating, impulsing. Or again, a Christian is one in whom Christ is formed, through whom Christ is manifested, with whom Christ cooperates, and to whom Christ grants a fellowship in His sufferings.

All these truths lie in germ in the incidental—I do not

ITS NATURE

think accidental—use of the word "Christian" in the New Testament. Granted the primal fact of the indwelling Christ, the three facts suggested always result. The indwelling Christ masters the life, and reveals Himself through the mastered life. The indwelling Christ creates the new desire, the new aspiration, the new passion, that drives the one indwelt along the path of service. The indwelling Christ gives new satisfaction in purity, and makes it impossible for the one indwelt to share in the things of evil, and so brings upon that one the very reproach that rested upon the Lord Himself.

It is seen therefore, and I do not think we can be too careful in emphasizing this, that Christian life is neither human imitation of Christ, nor correct intellectual positions concerning Christ. Neither is it a cult, or a system of thought. I may attempt to imitate Christ very sincerely through long years, and yet never be a Christian. I may hold absolutely correct intellectual views concerning Christ as a Person, and His power, and yet never be a Christian. It is possible for me to admire Him, and to attempt with all the power of my life to imitate Him, and yet never realize Him. Yet let it be speedily added, no one has ever attempted this without learning the impossibility of the task. Any person continuing long in an attempt to imitate, merely proves by such action that the Christ has never really been seen. To see Him in all the perfection of His character, and the radiant splendour of His personality is at once to recognize the absolute futility of all attempts to imitate Him.

Neither is the nature of the Christian life that of holding the truth about Christ. It is quite possible for a person to believe most sincerely in His Deity, and in the fact of His atoning work; and moreover, in the necessity for regeneration; and yet never be submitted to His Lordship, never to have personal share in the work of His atonement, never to be born again.

Nothing short of the coming into the life of the individual of Christ Himself constitutes a Christian.

If Jesus Christ is external to your life there will be moments when the world will not see Him and hear Him, and will not know you belong to Him. But if Christ be in you, living, reigning there absolutely, and you are obeying Him, there never will be a moment when the truth will not be evident. You cannot hide Christ if once He comes within. If the light be there, it simply must shine. There is no such thing as long continued secret discipleship. Nicodemus will be a secret disciple, and so will Joseph of Arimathæa, but when the crisis comes, and all the rest have run away, they will beg the Master's body, and bear it tenderly to the burial.

There is an application of a saying of Jesus, which while not the immediate one intended, is nevertheless true to the principle involved. "Except a corn of wheat fall into the earth and die, it abideth by itself alone; but if it die, it beareth much fruit." There is of course no doubt that Christ here referred to Himself, and to the fact of His approaching death. Take the figure, however, and think of it for a moment quite apart from its setting, and as revealing principles at once simple and sublime. In a corn of wheat there is the very principle of life, and therefore the possibility of a great harvest. It lies within the grain in potentiality, but there can be no harvest until that grain is sown, and passing through death, it emerges into the manifold life. Two things are required, first there must be the grain, but secondly the grain must be planted. If there is to be a harvest of Christian character in individual life, there must first be the grain, containing the life principle. It is not enough to have the germ principle in mind and intellect. It must be planted in the life. Christ must be formed within by the communication of Himself, first in the realm of identification with His death on the Cross, and then in the spacious glory of union with Him in the triumph of His resurrection.

Here we have reached the realm of mystery, and it is quite conceivable that some enquiring heart will say, How can these things be? By such question two things may be intended. If the question be as to what are the conditions upon which these things may be, it can be answered. If on the other hand, the question ask the explanation of the process of the Spirit in the communication of the Christ life, there is no answer. None can perfectly understand that act of the Spirit of God in which He communicates to the individual soul the very Christ life itself. That it is done upon certain conditions is however absolutely certain, and moreover, the conditions are clearly stated. In that moment when the soul submits to the claim of Christ, Christ is formed within by the Holy Spirit. Directly there is submission to Him as the absolute Lord of life, and trust reposed in Him for the putting away of sin, and for the communication of life; then, by a process utterly beyond the explanation of men, the Spirit communicates Christ's life, and Christ begins to live and reign and work in the soul of the submitted and trusting one. There can be no simulation of this life of Christ. It must be Christ in us. Holiness is not *it*. It is *Him!* Purity is not an abstract quality communicated as apart from Christ. It is Christ in the life, "breathing through the pulses of desire, His coolness and His balm," quenching passion's fires, and lighting the new fires of God, and of holy aspiration.

Now are you inclined to say, That does not satisfy me? I cannot be a Christian because I cannot understand the process? Then I would remind you that you are asking for something in the matter of the Christian life that you never ask for in any other realm. Do you refuse to submit to Christ because you do not understand how Christ's life, and Christ's purity can be communicated to you? Then on the same basis you must refuse to love flowers, for you cannot understand the mystery of the life of a flower. It is not merely in this fact of the Christ life that there is mystery. No man has ever yet explained the mystery of the simplest form of life. What is life after all? It is said that a German chemist sat in his laboratory for forty years engaged in one experiment alone. Was he successful? Never! For forty years he attempted to take the constituent parts of matter, and so to mix them as to produce life. Analyzing the germ he declared he found carbon, oxygen, nitrogen, and hydrogen, and he imagined that if he could only find the proper proportion of these, life would be the result, but he never succeeded. Life is a mystery. It cannot be explained.

So also in this Christian fact. The communication of the Christ life is full of mystery, and I pray you, ever distrust the man who imagines he perfectly understands it. A mystery truly, and yet a fact demonstrated by the experience of centuries. Take but one illustration. Here is a life mastered by evil passion, that life is brought to Christ, submitted to Christ. With what result? It is wholly changed, and that by an internal power, surprising the man himself, as he finds himself mastered by a new life which in turn makes him master of the very things that have held him in bondage. That is the real nature of Christianity. Wherever a soul submits to Christ, Christ passes into actual possession of the life, and an existence begins which is entirely new, and which is in perfect harmony with the Christ Himself.

Under the control of the indwelling Christ a man becomes a disciple, and the men of Antioch, or any other city, will say, That is a Christian. Under the control of the indwelling Christ he begins to live in order to lead people to Christ, and Agrippa, or other men will say, Wouldest thou persuade me to be a Christian? And he will answer, Yes, that is the passion of my being. Under the constraint of the indwelling Christ he will be delivered from the evil things around, and there will come to him the reproach of Christ, and he will not be ashamed, but glory rather in that reproach.

The nature of Christianity is Christ in the life, and therefore I make this appeal. Do not attempt to be a Christian by correcting the circumference of your life. Let Christ come into its centre, and He will correct the circumference. You cannot make a circle by commencing with the circumference. You must first set one foot of your compass at the centre. It is said that only one artist ever produced a perfect circle, and perhaps the round O of Giotto was after all but a freak. In the spiritual realm to work at the circumference of things for their correction is the utterest folly. Let Christ be the living Centre, and the life under His control will be corrected in all the sweep of its circumference. The nature of the Christian life is Christ. To that nothing can be added.

THE LIFE OF THE CHRISTIAN-
ITS SUSTENANCE.

"Break Thou the bread of life,
 Dear Lord, to me,
As Thou didst break the loaves
 Beside the sea;
Beyond the sacred page
 I seek Thee, Lord;
My spirit pants for Thee,
 O living Word!

Bless Thou the truth, dear Lord,
 To me—to me—
As Thou didst bless the bread
 By Galilee;
Then shall all bondage cease,
 All fetters fall;
And I shall find my peace,
 My All-in-All!"
—Mary A. Lathbury.

"Father, supply my every need,
 Sustain the life Thyself hast given,
Call for the never-failing bread,
 The manna that comes down from heaven."
—C. Wesley.

"Man, earthy of the earth, an hungered feeds
 Of earth's dark poison tree—
Wild gourds, and deadly roots, and bitter weeds;
 And as his food is he.
And hungry souls there are, that find and eat
 God's manna day by day—
And glad they are, their life is fresh and sweet,
 For as their food are they."
—G. T. S.
"Hymns of Ter Steegen, Suso, and Others."

CHAPTER II.

THE LIFE OF THE CHRISTIAN—ITS SUSTENANCE.

"Verily, verily, I say unto you, He that believeth hath eternal life. I am the bread of life. Your fathers ate the manna in the wilderness, and they died. This is the bread which cometh down out of heaven, that a man may eat thereof, and not die. I am the living bread which came down out of heaven; if any man eat of this bread, he shall live for ever: yea, and the bread which I will give is My flesh, for the life of the world." John vi. 47-51.

"Howbeit when He, the Spirit of truth, is come, He shall guide you into all the truth: for He shall not speak from Himself; but what things soever He shall hear, these shall He speak: and He shall declare unto you the things that are to come. He shall glorify Me: for He shall take of Mine, and shall declare it unto you." John xvi. 13-14.

"Let the word of Christ dwell in your richly." Col. iii. 16.

"Be filled with the Spirit." Eph. v. 18.

The word life suggests development. Arrest placed upon the development of life surely results sooner or later in its cessation. The Christ life is not a factor held separately from the believer's life. It is my veritable life if I am indeed a Christian. There are certain methods of speech and of thinking, which may sometimes be interpreted into the false idea that a Christian is one who has a personality separate in some way from his Christian life, that the Christ life is a deposit, something given to him in some mysterious way for him to guard, and yet separate from him. Hence we hear of the doctrine of the two natures. I am not proposing to discuss that doctrine here and now. There may be an element of truth in it, but it is perfectly certain that the Christ life is not something in me, separate from me, of which I have to take care, and of which if I do take care I am saved notwithstanding myself. The Christ life in the believer is his own life. There are forces in the will, the emotion, and the intellect, which need to be brought by patient perseverance under the control, but the life of the Christian is that of the Christ. That is what the apostle surely meant when he wrote, "I have been crucified with Christ; and it is no longer I that live, but Christ liveth in me: and that life which I now live in the flesh I live in faith, the faith which is in the Son of God, Who loved me, and gave Himself up for me." "Not I—but Christ liveth in me." The same personality, but a new life, a new impulse, a new reason, a new force, a new outlook. The life of the apostle was the Christ life. The Christ life was the life of the apostle.

If indeed the life we received when we abandoned ourselves to Christ was Christ's life imparted by the Spirit, the issue must be that our life will grow into the likeness of Him Whose life is now the dominating force within us. Every day should show some approximation in character and conduct to Christ Himself.

While it is perfectly true that the Christ life in the believer will grow and develop, bringing all the territory of the personality under its sway, and power, and control; yet it is equally true that there is a responsibility resting on the believer, certain laws of life which must be obeyed. And the first is that of securing proper sustenance. Created life, from a flower to an archangel, is dependent for the sustenance of life upon forces outside itself. All resources lie within the mystery of Deity, but God alone is Self-sufficient. In other words, the creature makes demands upon the Creator for the preservation of the life which He has caused to be, and in the economy of God there is perfect provision for the sustenance of all life which He has created.

Therefore my life in Christ is not self-sufficient. It is only as it receives from the outside that it can continue and develop. As in the physical life of man, so in the spiritual, there are two elements of necessary sustenance, proper food, and proper atmosphere. Both the food of the Christian, and the atmosphere in which he is to live are indicated in the passages at the commencement of this chapter. Christ says, "He that believeth hath eternal life. I am the bread of life." That is to say, that He is the sustenance of the life we have received from Him. The Christ life can only be fed by Christ. Not by something He gives me as apart from Himself, not by blessings He bestows upon me, but by the fact that the values and the virtues and the victory of His life are mine in Him, and are all available for the sustenance of His life in me.

Christ then, is the bread of life, and the soul having received the life of the Christ, is now to be fed and sustained by Christ. The atmosphere of the life is the Holy Spirit in all His powers. Neither of these means of sustenance can be neglected without peril to Christian life. In the full use of both, there will be constant development and growth without effort or undue consciousness.

In order to an understanding of the nature of this

heavenly bread, let us think first of the perfections of the Person of Christ, and then of the provision of His propitiation, and finally of the programme of His purpose.

First as to the perfection of His Person. Christ is the realization and manifestation in history of the essential facts in Deity which are necessary for the sustenance of spiritual life. In Christ the world has had the one and only revelation of the absolute perfection of human life. It is remarkable, and never to be forgotten that even those who have not been able to receive certain truths about Christ that we hold as fundamental and most dear, yet acknowledge the absolute beauty and perfection of His character. Jesus said, "Which of you convinceth Me of sin?" and that question still challenges the ages, and has never been answered except in the way in which Pilate expressed himself when he said, "I find no fault in Him." Books intended as criticisms of Christ invariably recognize the beauty of the ideal realized in His life. Strauss affirmed that the story of Jesus must be a myth, for no such human life was possible, because it was too sweet, too glorious, too beautiful. The brilliant Frenchman, Renan, has given us one of the most marvelous pictures of the human Christ on record. These men denying revealed truth concerning the Person of Christ, have yet through contemplation of the picture revealed in the Gospels, recognized Him as *facile princeps* among the sons of men.

The notes of the perfection of Jesus are very many. And here one can only utter broken sentences. Think of the perfections of that Person, the absolute perfection of Deity in that Person, the absolute perfection of humanity in that Person. This mystery is infinitely beyond comprehension, and consequently it is infinitely beyond explanation. There is no essential of Deity that is not manifested in the record of these four Gospels. And yet there is no essential of human nature—sin apart, which is not an essential—there is no essential of human nature that is not manifested also. Infinite wisdom in many of the things He said, human limitation in a few of the things He uttered. Infinite strength dominating all His life, and yet human weakness, making Him tired when the day's work was over.

Think of that spirituality, which was a perfect consciousness of God, and which enabled Him to touch all life here familiarly. Think of that submissiveness of Spirit, which was always under the control of God. Think of that keen and quick sympathy which enabled Him to project His own consciousness into that of others, so that in the sorrow of others He was sorrowful, and in their joy He was joyful. Think of that marvelous strength that made Him the unhesitating One, never deliberating, never perplexed, never wondering; but with calm sure tread, marching through all the difficulties and obstacles of life, until at last He uttered in quiet and dignified assertion the words, "All authority hath been given unto Me." These are simply notes of the perfections of the Christ, not now fully examined, but to be remembered as evidences of His perfection.

Then the great plan of His propitiation, that marvelous work by which He has opened the kingdom of heaven to all believers, and through which He takes hold of utter failure, and turns it into glorious success. His pardon for the sinner upon the basis of righteousness, His purity for the impure, by the communication of life. His peace

c

and power and promise, that light the darkest day with glory. All this comes within the compass of His work, and all is at our disposal, and part of the sustenance of our spiritual life.

The utterance of philosophic science which reveals the measure of its conclusions during the last half century, is the doctrine of the survival of the fittest. I do not deny the accuracy of this deduction from observations made. It undoubtedly has in it a great element of truth. Jesus Christ however, in the dawn of this new century, again faces men in the hopelessness born of such a philosophy, and declares to them that He came not merely to aid in the strengthening of the fit, but principally for the salvation of the unfit. Just at the point where human science and human philosophy break down, Christ enters; and by the pathway of His perfect life, and the mystery of His atoning death, and the victory of His triumphant resurrection takes hold of human life, and saving man, enables him to do the things he could not do, and makes him master of the forces that have mastered him. Christ is a perfect Saviour because He is a perfect Person, Who through the process of the suffering of His death has provided a new force for the remaking of the ruined.

And finally, the great programme of His purpose, which is the utter and final salvation of man, the lifting up to Himself of everything in human life, the building up of a God-redeemed society, the reconciliation of all things to God in this age, and in the ages to come, in the heavens, and in the earth. Salvation does not merely mean that a human being is saved from the punishment of sin to find the way into the after-glow of glory. It means all that, but it is also the process by which everything in human life, as created by God, is to be found and realized and crowned to the glory of God, in the perfecting of man.

These are the great facts, feeding upon which the new life of the soul is to be strengthened and sustained. Christ is not a small matter! All the infinite mystery, and the radiant majesty, and the overwhelming magnificence of that Person are for us.

The question may now be asked, How is the soul to feed upon Christ? How are these things to become ours, not merely intellectually, but to enter into the fibre of the being, and to remake us? Three words mark the method of the soul's feeding upon Christ—contemplation, meditation, and dedication. First, the contemplation of Christ, then meditation upon the things seen, and finally the yielding of the life to the claim which always lies within the vision granted, the dedication of the life to Him.

Christ is the bread of life. We are to feed upon Him. To this end our first responsibility is that of contemplation. There must be time taken to "consider Him." What a suggestive word that is. We must contemplate Him. We must see Him. We must know Him. We must make ourselves acquainted with Him. This is perhaps the most restless age that has ever been. Oh, the passionate movement of it, how it catches us, and sweeps us along ere we know it. Its perils are great, and constantly amid the stress and strain of work we long for those days of old, when it was possible to get away from life's activity, and spend some time in lonely contemplation of the Lord and Master. How little time we spend in quiet earnest effort of contemplation. In this connection it must be remembered that the fact of life is of supreme importance. Any attempt to see Christ, even in the Word, without the gift of life, will prove abortive. It is possible to study the New Testament intellectually and sytematically, and never to see Jesus Christ. For the proper reading and interpretation of the inspired Book it is necessary that there should be inspired readers. If we are Christ's and the Christ is in us, then the inspiration of His inward presence will enable us to see Him in the Word as we read it; and it is that contemplation of Him in the place of quietness and submission that is necessary if we are to feed upon Him, and He is in growing measure to become our very own.

Then secondly there must also be meditation, the thinking in the presence of the thing seen, and the bringing of the truth and the glory we have looked at into immediate relationship with all the details of our every-day life. As the glory of Christ breaks out upon the waiting soul, we must hold ourselves in the light of the glory, until the glory searches and tries us. Our life must be measured by His life, and it is a part of the process of the soul's sustenance that we should take time to set all our life in the light of the glory and beauty of His.

And yet once more, there must be added to contemplation and meditation, honest and whole-hearted dedication. It is impossible to spend even an hour with Christ without being rebuked. The vision of His glory seen, must always reveal the shortcoming, the failure of our own life. It is impossible to commune with Him without hearing His voice calling to something higher than anything already realized. And we must answer the claim that comes when the vision is seen, by obeying at all costs. Those who know Christ the best are most conscious of the infinite wealth, the infinite glory not yet explored; and perpetually to the soul who considers Him, and meditates in His presence, there will come the sound of His voice calling to something higher, to follow Him into yet larger realization of Himself. So when our attitude is that of a constant dedication, an every-ready answer to the claim of each new outbreak of glory from the Person of Christ, we shall feed upon Him, take Him into our being in ever-increasing measure, and as He thus is formed in us, we shall grow up into Him in all things.

Before turning from this first thought concerning the food of the Christian life, let it be remembered that there are two things necessary, regularity and system. To contrast our habits in the matter of physical and spiritual feeding, will often be to reveal the reason of the weakness of our spiritual life. Some people seem only to feed upon Christ on Sunday, imagining that this is all they need of spiritual food. Others only give themselves to such feeding upon Christ when affliction overtakes them. The result is that occasional and spasmodic communion with Christ results in like manifestation of Christian character. It is far more important that the Christian should feed on Christ regularly than that the physical life should be cared for. If on the morning of any given day through press of circumstances, there is only time for one thing, the meal which supplies the necessities of the body, or the hour of communion which sustains the strength of the spirit, the breakfast should be abandoned, and the time of fellowship retained. It may safely be affirmed that where this rule is observed, the breakfast is seldom omitted from the programme of the day.

Moreover this feeding on Christ should not be relegated

to special occasions. There is a great tendency to attend conventions and conferences for the sustenance of Christian life, under the impression that such special occasions will supply all that is necessary, perhaps, for a year. It is not by great banquets that physical life is maintained, but by quiet and regular supply of necessities. So also great conferences or conventions will by no means take the place of regular contemplation, meditation, and dedication. Feeding upon the bread of life must be a perpetual process if indeed we would grow into the likeness of Christ.

Moreover, there should be system in this matter, and here is the true work of the pastor and teacher, that of leading the sheep of the pasture into that particular part thereof which is most adapted to their age, capacity, and requirement. Every church should be one great Bible school, and the minister's supreme function that of teaching the Word, and so feeding the flock of God. This cannot be done by the preparation of literary disquisitions on philosophical subjects, but by careful, systematic, constant study of the Word of God, and its exposition and enforcement in the companies of the saints.

The question of atmosphere is quite as important as that of food. The Christian must live in the true atmosphere, which is the fellowship of the Spirit. There is no essential difference between the indwelling Christ and the indwelling Spirit. These two phrases reveal complementary aspects of one truth. The Spirit's indwelling reveals the Christ, and thus Christ indwells us by the Spirit. Yet if we are to understand the laws of our life, we are bound to recognize the personality and work of the Holy Spirit. When His disciples were gathered around Him, just before His departure, Jesus breathed on them, an action at once prophetic and symbolic, indicating the Holy Spirit as the living link between Himself and those disciples. The Spirit of the Christ outbreathed by the Christ and inbreathed by the believer, becomes the link between the believer and the Christ, between the Christ life in all its fullness, and the need of the believer.

The true atmosphere, therefore, of the new life is that of the Spirit of God. Life in the Spirit is life in the atmosphere which will enable us to see the Christ, to understand Him, to dedicate ourselves to Him.

The method of the Spirit may be indicated again by three words, revelation, explanation, transformation. The Spirit first reveals Christ. As the vision is seen, the Spirit explains its meaning, and applies it to the necessities of life. As the vision is obeyed, the Spirit transforms the obedient one into the likeness of the Christ revealed.

These two sets of three words stand over against each other. The Spirit's revelation of Christ answers the attitude of contemplation. The Spirit's explanation of the revelation answers our meditation on that revealed glory. The Spirit's transformation answers our dedication of ourselves to the explanation of the revealed glory.

Jesus said of the Spirit, "He shall take of Mine, and shall declare it unto you." The work of the Spirit is to reveal Christ. He has nothing to say to us about Himself. All that was necessary to be said concerning Him, Christ Himself said. The method of the Spirit is at once simple and sublime. Christ in all His glory can never be revealed to any one individual at any moment. Through processes marked by infinite patience, the Spirit reveals this infinite glory of the Lord "line upon line, precept upon precept." Such revealing is made to those given to contemplation. Every new manifestation of the Master's glory is granted that we may ponder it, gaze upon it, look deeply into it. While thus occupied the Spirit continues His gracious work. He opens the mind and heart that we may understand the vision. This explanation is the Spirit's response to earnest meditation, applying the light and glory to all the recesses of our life, and to all the habits and conduct of the days. Such exercise will ever mean, as we have said before, the revelation of things to be corrected, and of new duties to be undertaken. Here is our supreme point of responsibility. If for fear, or in response to selfish motives, we fail to obey, we grieve the Spirit; and not until there has been repentance and obedience will any further vision be granted. If on the other hand, we dedicate ourselves to the light by obeying its call, the Spirit completes the gracious process of His operation by transforming us into that which we have seen of Christ, and obeyed.

Take one illustration only. In some moment when the heart is set upon Christ in contemplation, the Spirit reveals the fact of His compassion. In my own experience the most startling revelation that ever came to me of Christ was this revelation of His compassion. I can never forget the hour when the words, "He was moved with compassion," long familiar as words, and as a general declaration of a truth, flamed out, and flashed, and burned with a new light and meaning that I had never seen before. When such revelation comes, it is ever the work of the Spirit, and our duty is not to withdraw ourselves from the fierce light, even though it scorch us for our failure, but rather should we force ourselves into its clearest shining, even though we be filled with shame at the selfishness which has characterized even our service. So surely as the soul thus responds to the light, the Spirit will make that very compassion of Christ part of the experience of the one thus yielded, and a new and yearning tenderness over all the lost will prove the realization in character of the compassion of Christ, as a new impulse of life and service.

So also with His purity, and with everything in the glorious perfections of His person, His passion, and His power. We contemplate, the Spirit reveals. We meditate, the Spirit explains. Then we answer with new dedication, and the Spirit transforms us into the realization of the truth revealed. So life grows into the likeness of Jesus Christ.

The relation of these two facts in the sustenance of the spiritual life is as close as is the relation of atmosphere to food in the realm of the physical. We know that physical life cannot be maintained apart from proper sustenance and fresh air. Shut a person off from air, and he will soon lose his appetite, and sicken, and die, even though the best of food be provided. There must be, and there is in Christ, perfect provision for the strengthening of the Christ life in the believer. And yet this can only be appropriated as the child of God lives in such relation with the Spirit of God as fulfills the apostolic injunction, "Grieve not the Holy Spirit."

The two complementary injunctions in the Colossian and Ephesian epistles reveal most clearly the inter-relation between these two phases of the subject of sustenance. The Word of Christ, standing for all the wealth of His glory, must dwell in us. That can only be as we are filled with the Spirit Whose sacred office it is to interpret to us and realize within us the facts and forces of the life of Christ.

The life of the Christian is the Christ life. So far as our will and responsibility are concerned there must be personal feeding on Christ, and in order to this we must live in the atmosphere of the Spirit exclusively. As there must be no neglect of the bread of heaven provided, so also must there be no descent to the malarial valleys. Life must be lived on the mountain heights in unceasing relation to the Spirit, Who is the one and only Interpreter of Christ.

Some years ago I met in the south of England a dear friend, and looking at him was filled with sorrow as I saw at once that he was in the grasp of that insidious disease which with deadly certainty saps away the life. After a long interval when I was in Colorado, I saw him again, and hardly knew him. The rare air of the mountains had given him back his old strength, and had made impossible the spread of his disease. He told me however that while feeling perfectly well, it was necessary for him to stay upon those mountain heights, or the old trouble would return.

Let us keep ever in the mountain air. If we descend into the old valleys, the paralysis of the past will come again. We must live in the atmosphere of the Spirit, high on the mountains of vision, and there the appetite for the bread of heaven will be strong, and feeding upon Christ we shall "grow up into Him in all things."

"Let the word of Christ dwell in you richly." "Be filled with the Spirit." Do not let us treat these words, and this study as theories merely, to be discussed and understood intellectually. From this day forward let us, as never before, take time to contemplate, to meditate, and to dedicate; these all moreover, in perpetual relation to the Great Spirit of God Who grants the vision of the Christ, and realizes in all submissive souls His glorious victories.

THE LIFE OF THE CHRISTIAN—ITS EXPRESSION.

"Who live, O God, in Thee
    Entirely Thine should be;
Thine we are, a heaven-born race,
    Only to Thy glory move,
Thee with all our powers we praise,
    Thee with all our being love."
—C. Wesley.

"I want an even strong desire,
    I want a calmly-fervent zeal,
To save poor souls out of the fire,
    To snatch them from the verge of hell,
And turn them to a pardoning God,
    And quench the brands in Jesus' blood.

I would the precious time redeem,
    And longer live for this alone,
To spend, and to be spent, for them
    Who have not yet my Saviour known;
Fully on these my mission prove,
    And only breathe, to breathe Thy love.

* * * * * *

Enlarge, inflame, and fill my heart
    With boundless charity divine!
So shall I all my strength exert,
    And love them with a zeal like Thine;
And lead them to Thy open side,
    The sheep for whom their Shepherd died."
—C. Wesley.

CHAPTER III.

THE LIFE OF THE CHRISTIAN—ITS EXPRESSION.

"Whosoever shall confess that Jesus is the Son of God, God abideth in him, and he in God. And we know and have believed the love which God hath in us. God is love; and he that abideth in love abideth in God, and God abideth in him. Herein is love made perfect with us, that we may have boldness in the day of judgment; because as He is, even so are we in this world." I. John. iv. 15-17.

Granted that the life of the Christian is the Christ life communicated by the Spirit, and that the sustenance of Christian life is Christ apprehended by the Spirit, it follows that the expression of the Christ life will be Christ. This John states superlatively in the words, "As He is, even so are we in this world."

It is questionable whether there is any statement in the New Testament quite as startling in this particular connection as this of the beloved apostle. It is so startling that we are compelled to face and examine it as to its context before considering it in itself. We do not propose to deal fully with the whole argument of the apostle. These especial words, "As He is, even so are we in this world," constitute the declaration of a great fact, and it is announced here because of its bearing on the argument in which the apostle is engaged. We can only enter fully into the meaning of the declaration as we have at least a general understanding of the wider truth being dealt with.

The apostle is occupied with the great subject of a manifested life, of a new quality of life, which he speaks of as eternal life. Yet he never deals with it in the abstract, but always as revealed in the Person of Jesus Christ.

Going back only as far as the statement immediately preceding our text, "Herein is love made perfect with us," there has been a difference of opinion as to what the word "herein" refers to, as to which is cause and which is effect. Does the "herein" refer to what has gone before it, or to that which immediately follows? Does the apostle mean to say that love is made perfect with us through the consciousness of the fact that we have boldness in the day of judgment because of our likeness to Christ; or does he mean to say that our love is made perfect in the fact that God abideth in us, and that because of this we have boldness in the day of judgment; and that moreover, on account of the fact that "as He is, even so are we in this world?" Personally I believe that the latter is the correct exegesis of the text. The "herein" refers to that which has been already stated. "God is love, and he that abideth in love abideth in God, and God abideth in him. Herein"—in this mutual interabiding, abiding in love, that is, our abiding in God, and God abiding in us, in that supreme and marvelous inter-relation—"is love made perfect with us."

That being so, we may examine the statement itself. "As He is, even so are we in this world." Our first question is, Who is "He?" The "He" here undoubtedly refers to Christ. John constantly referred to the Master by the use of the personal pronoun, and sometimes by the expression "that One." It is a peculiar characteristic of his writings, especially noticeable in the epistles. There are occasions when without naming Christ, without even using the personal pronoun, it is most certain he is making reference to Him. For instance, he writes in one place that we "ought to walk as He"—literally, "as that One walked."

An explanation of this method of the apostle is to be found in the fact that he wrote with his eyes perpetually resting upon the Lord Christ. He opens this epistle, "That which was from the beginning, that which we have heard, that which we have seen with our eyes, that which we have beheld, and our hands handled, concerning the Word of life . . . that which we have seen and heard." In every case the word "that" refers to Christ, and suggests the method of a man who writes with the Person of Christ filling his vision. If there is a phrase which describes that which cannot be seen, or heard, or handled, it is the phrase, "the Word of life." The phrase suggests that which is intangible, imponderable, something that cannot appeal to the ordinary senses. and yet John writes clearly that this Word of life was manifested to men in the Person of Him to Whom the same apostle refers in the opening of his great Gospel when he wrote, "In the beginning was the Word, and the Word was with God, and the Word was God. And the Word became flesh, and tabernacled among us (and we beheld His glory, glory as of the only begotten from the Father), full of grace and truth." So that the supreme revelation of life, of eternal life has been granted to us in the Person of Jesus Christ.

D

The writings of John are not in some senses as doctrinal as those of Paul. His argument is never as conclusive, and the logical element is almost entirely absent. Paul is the great logician. John is the great interpreter. Paul leads us along the line of stately argument until our reason is compelled to acquiesce. John presents to our mind and heart a great vision, and we are convinced without argument. I do not desire to place these men in conflicting contrast, for their method is complementary, and they give us the two sides of the great whole of conviction. John's reference then in the words, "As He is, even so are we in this world" is to Christ.

Now we may ask a second question, "How is He? What did the apostle mean? The vision of Jesus to John was always that of Love incarnate. God is love, and Jesus is God revealed, consequently He is love revealed. We may reverently repeat the declaration in slightly altered form, "As He is love, even so are we love in this world." As the life of the Christian is the Christ life, and the Christ life is the love life, so the life of the Christian is the love life. When that is said, everything is said. We may attempt to see the different colours that commingle in a perfect harmony, making the essential light of life, but when we have said love, we have said all.

Tarrying yet a little with the text, before attempting to examine its application to practical life, and how love is therein expressed, notice carefully the form of the statement here, "As He is," not as He was. If it be true that John always wrote with his eye upon the human Christ, it is equally true that John always saw in the human Christ the eternal One. Notice how human Christ is to John. "We have seen . . . we have beheld . . . our hands have handled." Yet see how He is also the eternal, "The Word of life." Is it possible to handle the Word of life? Is it possible to see the Word of life? Is it possible to behold the Word of life? In these statements there is evidenced the great consciousness of John, two facts mingling and merging into a majestic unity, the fact of the human which is Divine; the revelation of the Divine expressing itself in human limitation. "As He is" not as He was. It is not the vision of the past, save as that serves to express the abiding present.

And again notice the tense is the same in the other sentence of the declaration, "so are we." Not, so shall we be. There is a sense in which we are not yet perfected into the likeness of Christ, and it is John who also says, "Now are we children of God, and it is not yet made manifest what we shall be. We know that, if He shall be manifested, we shall be like Him." That is the future tense, but there is a deep and present sense in which we are now like Him. "As He is," in the essence of His nature, "so are we" in the essence of our nature in Him. Because the statement is startling he reaffirms it by the addition of the words, "in this world." In the midst of the present economy, in the midst of the limitation of the processes of our education—using that word in its highest spiritual sense—even here and now, "as He is, even so are we."

We may now inquire how that Christian life expresses itself. When we yielded our poor life to Him, He gave His rich life to us, the life of love. How does it express itself in this world? The expression of the Christ life in the Christian is identical with the expression of the

Christ life in the Christ. Let us go back and contemplate Him during the days of His sojourn amongst men. While paying attention to the human, let us not forget that we are seeing the Divine.

We shall follow three lines of consideration. As we take our way through the world, we come into contact with God, and man, and the devil. Every day we live these touch us somewhere. What was the expression of the Christ life toward God? What was the expression of the Christ life toward man? What was the expression of the Christ life toward evil? By such contemplation shall we understand not what we ought to be, but what we are, and what we cannot help being, if we are wholly and absolutely yielded to Christ.

In each case we will take three words as expressing the facts. The Christ life expresses itself toward God in confidence, communion, and coöperation. The Christ life expresses itself toward man in sincerity, in sympathy, and in service. The Christ life expresses itself toward evil in antipathy, in antagonism, and in authority.

As to the first of these, is there anything more beautiful in the study of the life of our Lord, than His confidence in His Father, absolutely uninterrupted, absolutely unquestioning? The very key note of the music of the life of Jesus is to be found in that old time prophecy concerning Him, "I am come . . . I delight to do Thy will, O my God." As the life of the Christ passes in review before our minds we find that the whole of it is true to that first note of its music. It is the chord of the dominant, and you hear its tone running through all the harmonies. Confidence in God is faith in God. In the letter to the Hebrews, after the writer has given that marvelous scroll of the heroes and heroines of faith known and unknown, he says, Let us look at the supreme Witness, "Therefore let us also, seeing we are compassed about with so great a cloud of witnesses, lay aside every weight, and the sin which doth so easily beset us, and let us run with patience the race that is set before us, looking." At what? At the witnesses? No. "Looking unto Jesus." And why? "Who is the Author and Perfecter of faith." Not of our faith. The word our does not occur in the text, but "of faith" as a principle of life. The word Author very literally means file leader, that is, one who marches first in the procession, one who blazes the way through the forest, the pioneer of faith. The writer is holding Jesus of Nazareth up to the view of these men whose faith was wavering, these Hebrew Christians, because they thought that everything was lost as the old economy was passing away. He is telling them that more radiant than all the witnesses of the past is Jesus, the Exemplification of faith, the One Who has given the most perfect example of what the life of confidence or faith in God really is.

Then the word Finisher is also suggestive. We might substitute the word Vindicator as revealing the intention at this point. He most perfectly sets the pattern and proves the power. All through the life of Jesus this confidence in God is evident. His confidence appears to have been uninterrupted, unquestioning, and unbargaining. As far as the records reveal, Christ only once asked the question that we with our faltering faith so perpetually ask. He only once asked God "Why"? When in that awful mystery of the Cross He stood in my place, and suffered the veiling of the face of God, and passed into the mystery of the darkness incomprehensible, then He said, "My God, My God, why hast Thou forsaken Me?" We so often ask Why? Why must I bear this? Why must I go alone this rough pathway? Why have I been called to pass through these sorrows? I am not rebuking the question, for it comes up too often in my own heart. But by way of contrast come from the ofttime Why of men to the lonely Why of Jesus. With quiet calm strength He moved along the pathway of life, and all the duties and actions were true to that chord of the dominant struck ere the music was heard of man. Never until He stood in my place in all the depths and meaning of atoning agony, did He ask Why? His other sayings all breathe the spirit of a perfect confidence. "Know ye not that I must be about My Father's business?" "We must work the works of Him that sent Me." "I do always the things that are pleasing to Him." I have "accomplished the work which Thou hast given Me to do." "Father, into Thy hands I commend My Spirit."

That is the first expression of the Christ life toward God. "As He is, even so are we;" and that confidence will grow in proportion as we yield ourselves to the Christ, developing and enlarging every day.

Confidence merges into something more profound, communion with God. Perfect confidence in love creates the desire for fuller knowledge of love, and so the soul passes upon this basis of a perfect confidence into the region of a perpetual communion. There is a reflex action here. The more one trusts God, the deeper and the closer the communion with God becomes. Again consider the life of our Lord, and we shall see that His communion with

His Father was unbroken until that dark and mysterious hour of the Cross. In the lone vigils on the mountain side, in the nights spent in retirement from the thronging crowds, we find Him realizing the deepest experience of a communion with God which was perpetual. Do not imagine that Christ's communion with God was limited, that He only entered into communion when He left the crowd. He lived in communion. He was never out of the Divine presence consciously. His was a life homed in God. He lived and moved and had His being in God. That fact is most clearly stated by Himself. "I and My Father are one." Alone, "and yet I am not alone, because the Father is with Me."

And then finally, and because of these two facts, His life expressed itself in coöperation with God. The work of Jesus for God was never separated from the life of Jesus with God. The sense of the importance and the urgency of the Divine enterprises became the very passion of His life, and that whole life was therefore poured out an unbroken service. Jesus never rested from His work with God. He always rested in His work with God. Do not imagine that His work for the Father began with the Cross. That was simply the culmination, the final movement in one continuous coöperation with God. Every breath He drew was part of the force doing God's work. The very fact of His living was in itself coöperation with God.

That was the manifestation of Eternal Life in its expression toward God, and "as He is, even so are we in this world." This then is the expression of the life of the Christian. First confidence, that ever lies at the base of all fellowship with the Father.

> "They that trust Him wholly,
> Find Him wholly true."

We cannot try to trust God, but if Christ have His way, trust will deepen and broaden, and become profound. Yielded to the indwelling One, we shall find what it is to have perfect confidence in God, because of our understanding of His love.

From this foundation of confidence will come the life of communion. Communion means friendship, an interest in all the things of God, and a conviction of His interest in all the things of our lives. Communion will express itself in familiar intercourse, an intercourse in which each both speaks and listens. All the highest ideals of friendship are realized between the soul and God in communion. You remember the story of the old Scotch woman, whose minister was absent from his pulpit, and a stranger preached one Sunday. Somebody asked her how she had enjoyed the message of the stranger. "Oh," she said, "it was verra gude," but she strangely missed her own minister. When asked why, she uttered what I think was the rarest and most beautiful compliment ever paid to a minister. "Weel," she said, "it is not always what oor meenister says, but I never listen to our meenister without feeling he is so familiar with God." Oh, to be familiar with God. That is the completion and fruitage of communion.

In the actual experience of such communion the whole life becomes coöperation with God. There is nothing of greater importance than that we should understand this, that when we are living in true relationship with God, our whole life becomes coöperation with Him. A Christian cannot live without working for God. The life is the

ITS EXPRESSION

work. If we believe and understand this, we shall cease making false divisions between the secular and sacred, and shall no longer divide our lives into compartments, one for business, for pleasure, for home, for religion. Everything in the vocation in which you abide with God is coöperation with God, and with the great forces of God, for the bringing in of righteousness, and the establishment of His Kingdom.

Such is the Christ life in the Christ, and such is the Christ life in the Christian where the Christian is abandoned to the Christ. It may not be that we have perfectly realized experimentally all the truth, but it does mean that if the life of Christ is in us, we must test ourselves in the light of that revelation, and see what is our duty and responsibility.

Now let us consider what is the expression of the Christ life toward men. Three words again will help us, sincerity, sympathy, and service. What is sincerity? It is the simplicity of righteousness based upon the sublimity of love. Sincerity simply means perfect simplicity, not the simplicity of superficiality, but the simplicity of sublimity. Is there anything more true of the life of Christ than that of the simplicity of His dealing with men. There was no ulterior motive in what He said to men. There was no mental reserve when He talked to them. There was no double dealing in His methods with men. His whole attitude toward them was characterized by freedom from diplomacy, or subtlety. Jesus was the most transparent man that ever lived, clear as the light, simple as the line of truth. He was sincere, and therefore without offence in His dealings with men.

The Christian life always expresses itself in the same

way. It is based upon love, and there is no sentinel of righteousness so strict and stringent as love. To do right because of reputation, to do right because it is the correct thing, to do right to escape criticism, all such motives will fail sooner or later. To do right because I love is the one and only lasting motive. "Love never faileth."

And yet more, sympathy, the capacity for comradeship, the measure of freedom from self-consciousness, which gives me the consciousness of my brother's consciousness,

"A heart at leisure from itself,
To soothe and sympathize."

The measure of our ability to sympathize with someone else is the measure of our freedom from self-consciousness; and the measure of our freedom from self-consciousness is the measure of our love consciousness. Christ was surcharged with this. Sympathy characterized His attitude toward men. Every fibre of His being thrilled to essential love, and because of that He was self-forgetful. It would have been one great transport of delight to see the changes passing over His face. If a woman in trouble came near Him, He was troubled with her trouble. If a child played near Him, He played with the child. A recent writer has declared that Christ never smiled. Who told him so? There are some things so palpable as to be taken for granted, and so the Scripture makes no such declaration. Of course He smiled. No man incapable of smiling loves children, or can be loved by them. This Man took them in His arms, put one of them in the midst of His disciples, as a type and pattern of what their life should be. If you do not agree, then I cannot argue, but

I know this Man of love smiled often. If we had met Him in those days, He would have been joyful in our joy, or sad with our sorrow. And the measure in which Christ dwells in us, is the measure of our laughter with the man who laughs, and our rejoicing with such as rejoice, and our ability to enter into the realm of sorrow with those passing through its shadow.

The sympathy is practical, and becomes service. It is not a pity which weeps and passes on its way unhelping, but a pity that goes down to the need of the man with power to aid. Such pity is not idle. It is rather a mighty impulse to serve, and the measure of the service is sacrificial. The difference between the service which is Christly, and all other may be gauged by the cost to the man who is serving. We begin to express the Christ life when our service to humanity costs us something. It is possible for a very wealthy man without the Spirit of the Christ, to sign checks, but when the check is signed in blood, Christ is behind the signing. It is possible for a person to visit the slums of a great city, and return to sit in the midst of luxury, and write some article on How the poor live. But when a girl turns her back upon luxury, and dons the uniform of a Salvation lass, and lives in the slum, you may know that Christ lives in her. Until virtue goes out of the preacher, he has never preached. Until into our service there comes the element of the Cross, there is nothing of the Christ Spirit in the service.

And finally, the expression of the Christ life toward evil is first that of antipathy. The whole life of Jesus was a life of hatred of evil. He was able to say "The prince of the world cometh: and he hath nothing in Me." In His heart there lurked no hidden admiration of the things that were unlike God, and in His mind there was no approximation toward evil. You say, but here is the difference. And yet think again. You tell me you still love evil. I do not believe it. Are you truly a Christian? Then while it is perfectly true that evil may fascinate you, as it is presented to you in such guise as to be a temptation, yet get to the deepest fact of your life. All the while if Christ be there, you hate the thing which is fascinating you. You would give anything to be rid of it. Trust that profounder consciousness. Trust it, and yield to it. In the matter of evil the first evidence of the presence in you of the Christ is a dislike for it, an antipathy toward it. The proportion of our devotion to Christ, and of our submission to the inspiration of His life is the proportion in which we also lose our love for evil, and sin becomes a hateful thing.

This antipathy toward evil issues in antagonism. Here also we claim union with Christ. Christ definitely refused to let evil alone. So will every Christian. "The plea of evil" as Mr. Watkinson says, is "let us alone, Jesus Thou Son of God." This is its cry today, in the city, in the nation, in our own heart. "Let us alone," do not interfere with us. And the true Christian is always saying Come out. So surely as the Christ life is in us, with merciless, ruthless, and pitiless determination our life will be poured out in unceasing attack upon the strongholds of evil in the city, in the nation, in the home, and everywhere. In the wilderness Jesus said, "Get thee hence, Satan," and He will never cease His work until the enemy is finally cast out. If our life be Christ's life, then we can never sign a truce with evil. We cannot sit down and be indifferent to its presence.

And then thank God for the last word. The Christ life was that of authority over evil. Because Christ has won the battle already, the life of His follower shares His authority. It is most interesting to notice in the study of the life of Jesus that from that wilderness temptation on to the end, He never argued with the devil again. Whenever He came into contact with him, or with the evil spirits, it was with the tone of authority, and the authority was immediately obeyed. The Christ life in the believer sets him in antipathy to evil, and gives him a marvellous and mystic authority over it. If we will let Him speak through us, then He through us, and we through Him, can master every form of evil.

This then is the expression of the Christ life, and there can be no simulation of it. I cannot imitate it. It is possible to make flowers of wax, but the difference between them and the flowers of God that bloom and blow is the difference between the finite and infinite beauty. It is possible to paint a picture of some great landscape, but after all it is but a gathering of colours, and the flinging of them with genius upon a canvas; and the difference between the picture and the landscape is the difference between the copyist and the Creator. It is possible to imitate the Christian graces and virtues, but the difference between such imitation and the actual Christian life is the difference between base metal and the coinage of the kingdom of God. We cannot imitate this life. Our imitation will lack life. There may be some things which appear to be remarkable imitations of Christianity, but bring them and the Christ together, and you will at once find the infinite distance. There is only one way in which such life may be expressed, and that is by the indwelling Christ

Himself outworking all the beauties of His character through the duties and activities of the life of His child.

And yet a final word. Is the life present? Then let there be no discouragement because as yet the blossom and the fruitage are not perfect. First the blade, and then the ear, and then the full corn in the ear. Thank God if the blade be peeping above the brown soil today. It is the prophecy and potentiality of Christ-likeness which at last shall be found in perfection even in our lives.

THE LIFE OF THE CHRISTIAN—ITS CONSCIOUSNESS.

"Thrice blest is he to whom is given
  The instinct that can tell
That God is on the field when He
  Is most invisible.

Blest too is he who can divine
  Where real right doth lie,
And dares to take the side that seems
  Wrong to man's blindfold eye.

* * * * * *

For right is right, since God is God,
  And right the day must win;
To doubt would be disloyalty,
  To falter would be sin."
—Faber.

"Happy in knowing Thee, my Lord and God;
  Happy in finding Thee, my treasure true;
Happy in following Thee, through ill and good,
  In toiling for Thee, and in suffering too."
—Bonar.

"Blessed are the pure in heart,
  They have learned the angel-art,
While on earth in heaven to be,
  God, by sense unseen, to see.

Cleansed from sin's offensive stain,
  Fellowship with Him they gain;
Nearness, likeness to their Lord,
  Their exceeding great reward.

* * * * * *

Serious, simple of intent,
  Teachably intelligent,
Rapt, they search the written word,
  Till His very voice is heard.

* * * * * *

—W. M. Bunting.

CHAPTER IV.

THE LIFE OF THE CHRISTIAN—ITS CONSCIOUSNESS.

"Now the natural man receiveth not the things of the Spirit of God: for they are foolishness unto him; and he cannot know them, because they are spiritually judged. But he that is spiritual judgeth all things, and he himself is judged of no man. For who hath known the mind of the Lord, that he should instruct Him? But we have the mind of Christ." I. Cor. ii. 14-16.

"Father, the hour is come; glorify Thy Son, that the Son may glorify Thee: even as Thou gavest Him authority over all flesh, that to all whom Thou hast given Him, He should give eternal life. And this is life eternal, that they should know Thee the only true God, and Him Whom Thou didst send, even Jesus Christ. O righteous Father, the world knew Thee not, but I knew Thee; and these knew that Thou didst send Me; and I made known unto them Thy name, and will make it known; that the love wherewith Thou lovedst Me may be in them, and I in them." John xvii. 1-3.

"Have this mind in you, which was also in Christ Jesus." Phil. ii. 5.

The Christ life dominant in man will not only express itself in perfect harmony with the life of Jesus: it will also enter into His consciousness. In approaching this subject we must define the word consciousness. There is another word which we always strive to avoid in certain aspects of Christian work. It is the word feeling. In dealing with enquirers we urge them not to wait for feeling, but to exercise faith. But that is not to say that there is no feeling in the experience of Christianity. As a matter of fact there is a most definite consciousness which is peculiar to the Christian, and our present subject has to do with that.

The order of procedure in the Christian economy is first the fact, then faith taking hold of the fact, and finally, feeling growing out of the faith which takes hold of the fact. Whenever faith fastens upon the fact, feeling follows.

What then is this feeling, this consciousness of the Christian? Just as the life of the Christian is Christ, and the sustenance of the Christian life is Christ, and the expression of Christian life is Christ, so the consciousness of the Christian is that of Christ Himself. That is the whole answer. That is the essential light in which all the colours commingle. All I can do is to attempt to break the light up into some of its component parts. There is no music outside that name, no value apart from Him. When Christ dwells in a man, and the man's life is sustained by Him, He thinks, feels, and is conscious in that one.

In writing to the Thessalonian Christians the apostle speaks of their "whole spirit, soul, and body." That expression has been used to indicate the presence of a threefold fact in human personality. In some senses that is true. Perhaps the more correct way to state it would be to say that man is a spirit, indwelling a body, and having a mind or consciousness. The nature of this consciousness depends upon the relation which the body and the spirit bear to each other. It may be fleshly, it may be spiritual. The mind which is the centre of the being as to its consciousness, will reflect pre-eminently that which is regnant in the personality. Where the flesh reigns, the mind will be fleshly. Where the spirit reigns, the mind will be spiritual. In unregenerate man the consciousness is fleshly. The physical side of nature crowned and considered perpetually, the mind is necessarily fleshly. The regenerate man, on the other hand, is one in whom there has taken place the restoration of a Divine order, and his own spiritual nature is recognized as the supreme fact in his personality. Where this is so, the consciousness becomes spiritual. He looks at all things from the standpoint of the spiritual.

In writing to the Corinthians, the apostle makes a positive declaration, "we have the mind of Christ." In writing to the Philippians, he enjoins them "have this mind in you, which was also in Christ Jesus." The word "mind" in the first verse is not exactly the same word Paul used when he wrote "have this mind in you." It is in some senses a simpler word, meaning less, and yet in the present study of greater value. We shall do no violence to the real thought of the apostle if we substitute for "mind" the word "intelligence," "We have the intelligence of Christ." That is the sense in which we have the consciousness of Christ.

Thus we have here the statement of an essential fact, and an injunction to realize that fact in experience. This is the perpetual method of the apostle in urging Christians to the fulfilment of the ideal of the Christ life. He states a position with great clearness, and yet urges as a duty the realization of the truth declared. As on other occasions he says, "Ye have put off the old man . . . put off the old man;" "Ye have put on the new man . . . put on the new man;" so in bringing these two statements together, we adopt the same method. "We have the mind of Christ" . . . "Have the mind of Christ," which simply means, respond in experience to the fact of your privilege. Let the Christian who shares the Christ life, live the Christ life. Let the Christian who has the mind of Christ, have the mind of Christ.

"We have the intelligence of Christ." The apostle here quotes, adapting the literal form to the necessity of his own argument, the old time words,

> 'Things which eye saw not, and ear heard not,
> And which entered not into the heart of man.
> Whatsoever things God prepared for them that love Him."

These words are constantly quoted by Christians to prove that we cannot know these things,—a curious misquotation of Scripture. Read the context and you will find that Paul quotes it to show that that condition has passed away, that the Christian does know, for he goes on, "But unto us God revealed them through the Spirit." The apostle declares here that the natural man cannot know what the spiritual man does know, and that the consciousness which the natural man lacks, the spiritual man has. So that the great subject here is that of the Christian consciousness, the Christian intelligence, the Christian mind, which means more than intelligence, including also the emotion, and the will, that consciousness intellectual, emotional, volitional, which is the result of spiritual life and spiritual indwelling.

The purpose of the present study is that of examining this great fact. This is the surest way to the realization of the experience. In proportion as we have full knowledge of our privileges in Christ are we likely to abandon ourselves to all the glorious possibilities; and so realize our standing as a state.

In his epistle to the Philippians, after charging the saints that they have the mind of Christ, the apostle proceeds not so much to describe that mind, as to declare the activities that grow therefrom. The sublime passage which follows, describing as it does the coming of the Son of God from the high state of the eternal glory, down to the lowest level of man's degradation and need, constitutes an almost startling unveiling of the mind of Christ. As we watch with wonder and adoration the method of the Master, we discover His mind. As we examine the conduct of the Christ, we are made aware of His consciousness.

There can be but one thought uppermost in such a study. It is that of His love. Love is the active principle behind the great humiliation. But it may reverently be enquired, What lay at the back of the love, creating it? And perhaps the safest method of interpretation is that of listening to the statements of Christ Himself. For those which will help us most at this point, let us turn to the great intercessory prayer in which the Lord is speaking immediately to His Father. In the earlier sentences of the prayer He says, "And this is life eternal, that they should know Thee the only true God, and Him Whom Thou didst send, even Jesus Christ." At the close of the prayer we read again, "Oh righteous Father, the world knew Thee not, but I knew Thee; and these knew that Thou didst send Me; and I made known unto them Thy name, and will make it known; that the love wherewith Thou lovedst Me may be in them, and I in them."

Here carefully notice the sequence. Speaking of the revelation that He has made to His disciples He says, "I have made known unto them Thy name," and further affirms that the reason for this is that the love of God which He had for Christ may be in them. Then it is evident that at the back of the love consciousness was the knowledge of God. This harmonizes with that original word "This is life eternal, that they should know Thee the only true God." The supreme consciousness of Christ then, was the consciousness of God. Everything else was conditioned and included within this supreme knowledge. He was conscious of God supremely, over all, and under all, and in all, and through all. We may therefore consider this consciousness as objective and subjective, as the knowledge of God, and as the knowledge of everything else in relation to God.

The supreme intelligence of Christ was the intelligence of God, and therefore His knowledge of all other things, being related to that, was true knowledge, truth and never error, light and never darkness, nor even twilight. If He saw a flower, He saw God. If he saw a child, He saw God. If He saw the movements of His age, He saw God. Now this is not Pantheism. Jesus did not imagine that the flower was God. He did not think that the child was God, or even part of God. Wherever He looked, and whatever He saw, the supreme fact evident to His mind, underlying and enwrapping all works and words and thoughts was the God-consciousness.

This objective consciousness was manifest on every side of His personality. Intellectually, emotionally, and volitionally, His mind was conscious of God. Jesus of

Nazareth was a perfect instrument, perfectly adjusted for the perfect realization of God and truth. His intellect was unclouded, His emotion was undegraded, His will was perfectly poised and balanced in true relation to a supreme authority.

Think of the perfect consciousness resulting from that perfection of the instrument, so that God was intellectually apprehended. To the mind of Jesus the knowledge of God was not speculative or argumentative, but personal and immediate. He knew God not by the demonstration of an intellectual argument, but by personal contact and spiritual communion. It is worthy of notice that in all His preaching He never once argued for the existence of God. The great fact to Him was one that admitted of no denial, and therefore needed no defence. He never dreamed that there was any necessity to prove the existence of God. "My Father," "My Father," and the infinite music runs on through all the story of His life.

Then not only was God known to Him, He was emotionally apprehended by Him. He knew God as to His love. We take again the word which demonstrated the fact of His consciousness intellectually, and use it as in harmony with the emotional consciousness, "Father." It was not a new word, but it gained infinite meaning as He spoke it. It was not even a new word for God, for it was known long before He came in the flesh. Jesus so constantly used it in such varied circumstances that somehow it became radiant with new meaning, and whenever He said "Father," the very anthem of love broke upon the listening air. "The Son Who is in the bosom of the Father" was conscious of and actuated by, the love of God. All the great utterances in which He spoke of the Father to men, thrilled with the tenderness of the Divine heart.

And yet once more, not only was He intellectually and emotionally conscious of God, He was volitionally conscious of God. He knew that the will of God was the ultimate authority for all those created by God, their final court of appeal. He knew God is, that was intellectual apprehension. He knew He is Love, that was emotional apprehension. He knew He is King, that is volitional apprehension. Wherever He looked He saw God, whatever He listened to He heard God, wherever He found Himself He was in the presence of God.

We have the mind of Christ. This is eternal life, to know Him. It is varied, many sided, many coloured, having all kinds of expression. "Blessed are the pure in heart, for they shall see God." That this was so in the case of Christ becomes evident from the most casual survey of the story of His life. Whether in the commonplaces or the crises, in the small details or infinite duties, He is ever revealed as One Who is acting in the consciousness of the presence and power of His Father.

This objective consciousness of God necessarily issues in a subjective consciousness determined and dominated thereby. He was of course conscious of all the facts by which He was surrounded in life. And yet His consciousness of these was created and conditioned by His consciousness of God. Every form of being was seen by Him in relation to God as Origin. All purpose was seen by Him in relation to God as Love. And all realization was seen by Him in relation to God as King. What lay behind the universe to the mind of Christ?

God. What was the solution of the mystery of the earth? God. He looked into the face of a man, and what did He see? The image of God, even though that image was oftentimes defaced. Only spiritually enlightened eyes see that image as He saw it. He saw God everywhere, and the vision was interpretative of all else.

And not merely in these things, but in everything else. He saw God in human history. All movements were for Him tested by the relation they bore to God. Stretching out over all the affairs of individuals and of nations He saw the precise line of the Divine will and purpose, and that it was to be measured in its relation to God as Love. Jesus' was the true altruism, the true utilitarianism. Some people seem to want to divorce utilitarianism and beauty. Not so the Christ. In the true consciousness of God there is no divorce between these things. It has been said,

> "Straight is the line of duty,
> Curved is the line of beauty."

That is surely false. How far is it possible to draw a straight line without it becoming a curved one? Unless you are a believer in the flat earth theory, there is no straight line that does not curve into beauty. The final geometric symbol of God is the circle. "It is He that sitteth above the circle of the earth." And every line of duty that appears straight today, tramp it long enough, and it will grow into beauty. Christ saw that. He saw the purpose of love at the back of all the austerity and severity of law. His vision of the race was the vision of a commonwealth. Oh those little things He said that are so profound in their philosophy, "One is your

Teacher, and all ye are brethren." That is the true nation, the true commonwealth. The only true monarch and King is God's anointed King, and the race will never have its true commonwealth until He come. Christ was conscious of Love enfolding and enwrapping everything.

Then all realization of purpose was seen by Jesus in relation to God as King. Things were to be rejected according as they failed to coincide with that standard of requirement. All responding to Divine intention in character and conduct was satisfactory in itself and permanent. A man never finds real freedom of the will until he has found the seat of authority, and has put Christ there as King. Christ knew that. That was His meaning when He said, "Seek ye first His Kingdom and His righteousness, and all these things shall be added unto you."

This God-consciousness moreover, dominated the emotional side of His nature. It created in Him a great unrest, and an unending sorrow. His God-illumined intelligence, revealing the failure of all that harmonized with the Divine intention, created sorrow; because of the infinite love of the Father, which expressed itself in Him with unvarying insistence. In the presence of this failure there could be for Him no rest, no cessation of activity, no sitting in personal ease. "My Father worketh even until now, and I work," are words that reveal a Divine discontent with all that was unlike God. This discontent manifested itself occasionally in the tears that told of His anguish, and perpetually in the sacrificial service which characterized the busy years.

And yet again, contradictory as it may seem, this consciousness of God in the emotional nature gave Him an unbroken peace, and an unceasing joy. In the heart of this intercessory prayer, which was uttered when the shadow of the Cross fell over all His life, He prayed that His disciples might have His joy. How strange a petition it seems. He was pre-eminently in the presence of the world's sin and sorrow the Man of Sorrows; and yet the highest desire of His heart for men is that they may share His joy. This joy in the midst of sorrow was due to His consciousness of the ultimate victory of God in love over sin. Not only His intelligence, but His very heart was linked to the Throne of the Eternal. He knew God, and knew Him in all the majesty of His infinite and unfailing love. Thus, while there was ever a great sorrow in His heart, and a Divine discontent in the presence of sin, yet there was also a joy and content in the absolute assurance of the ultimate triumph of love.

And yet once more, and this is the sequence of what has already been considered, His will was always submissive to the will of God concerning all the things by which He was surrounded. Intellectually conscious of God, and certain of that Love which never failed, He was moreover conscious of the infinite wisdom and tender compassion and assured triumph of all the will of His Father. Therefore, with unswerving loyalty, He submitted Himself to that will, whether it chose for Him the path of sorrow or of joy, knowing right well that such wisdom and such Love could only choose the best, and must lead right onward to all highest victory.

This then is the mind that is in the Christian. The first and final consciousness of all those in whom Christ lives and reigns, is the consciousness of God. This may appear at first to be a statement which hardly harmonizes with experience, and yet a careful consideration will prove that it is actually true. In the light of such consideration we may be very much tempted to say that we have no such consciousness. We become submerged in the necessary duties of this life, and are ever surrounded by so many facts which appeal to us, that it would seem as though forgetfulness of God, rather than consciousness of Him, characterizes the experience of most of the days. It should, however, never be forgotten that perpetual consciousness of God does not necessarily mean actual thinking of Him in the surface activities of the mind. It is rather a perpetual and deep subconsciousness, which almost unconsciously, yet constantly, and effectively dominates other feelings, masters all impulses, and holds in check the surface activities of the mind.

There can be no finer illustration of it than the illustration of the constant consciousness of each other which exists between man and woman in the marriage relationship. They may often be separated from each other, and during the periods of separation will think of a thousand matters, and be busy in as many directions. Whole hours will pass in which the sacred relationship is not present to the surface of consciousness. And yet the relationship is never forgotten. It is a subconsciousness, holding all the life in relation to itself, and making impossible any deed, or word, or thought even, which is out of harmony with that supreme matter.

That is the true consciousness of every soul in whom Christ dwells. The immediate surroundings and conditions of the life of the Christian may be exactly what they were before relationship to Christ commenced. And yet they are absolutely different. Before the life was yielded to Christ the day was spent in the doing of certain routine duties in some schoolroom, or store, or office. That life will be continued. After it has been abandoned to Christ, the same duties have to be performed, the same kind of persons have to be dealt with, and yet the whole is radically changed. The old life was temporal, the new is eternal. In the past the duties had no relation to God. In the present every minutest detail is immediately related to Him. He in whom Christ dwells is conscious of God as Christ was conscious of God. To such an one a little child is no longer an interesting and playful animal, or even merely an undeveloped member of a human race, destined to get on in the world. It is rather one of those strange and marvellous beings whose angels always behold the face of the Father in heaven, rather than offend whom it were better that a mill-stone should be hanged about the neck, and the person offending drowned in the depth of the sea. When Christ is at the centre of the life men cannot be looked upon as they were. An unregenerate man, looking into the face of another man, sees in him an opportunity for his personal enrichment in some form. His question is, How much can I get out of that man? It may not always be money, but perhaps friendship, and love. Christ summarized the whole attitude in the words, "Ye love them that love you." But if Christ be in the life, then the question is an entirely new one, How much can I put into that man? How much can I do for him? The man is still there, but the God-consciousness creates an entirely new view of him.

Or again, a man of the world will pick up his newspaper, and see that two great powers are threatening to engage in an awful struggle, and he immediately thinks of the effect which will be produced upon the markets. A Christian man taking up his paper, and reading of such possibility, will think of widows, and orphans, and suffering, and sorrow.

And yet again in this same connection, the man of the world will feel in his heart a sense of panic in the presence of national struggle. But the man looking at all these things with the God-consciousness, will be at peace in the deepest fact of his life, for he will recognize the Divine movement, and will hear above the turmoil the voice of God saying, "I will overturn, overturn, overturn it . . . until He come Whose right it is; and I will give it Him." The one man looking only at the things seen may be troubled and perplexed, and speak of chaos. But the other from his consciousness of God, will be quiet and calm, as he is conscious of the certainty of the emergence of the cosmos from the chaos.

This supreme consciousness must have the effect of destroying everything that is low and mean and base. All littleness and meanness of motive become impossible to one to whom God is the all-inclusive fact. Conscious of God, a man has no place in his being for jealousy, criticism, cynicism. Nothing so broadens the outlook, and ennobles the impulse, and dignifies the conduct as a consciousness of God which illumines the intelligence, and conditions the emotion, and masters the will.

The measure in which Christ has possession of our lives is the measure in which our consciousness of God is keen and alert. If we find it necessary to defend the existence of God to our own hearts, or to remind ourselves occasionally and spasmodically of His government and His love, it is because we are failing to live in immediate fellowship with Christ Himself. It is impossible to force this consciousness. As a matter of fact, it is ours if indeed we have been born again of the Spirit of God. "We have the mind of Christ." He is the revelation of God to us. To know Him is to know God, and to know God is life eternal. Are there any two words which being brought together, mean quite the same as these two words? Life, eternal life! There is no narrowness in that. There is no meanness there. There is no selfishness, no cynical criticism, no little half-blind pessimism, no childish frivolity. Everything is spacious, free, infinite, grand, majestic. "We have the mind of Christ." Let it be ours by response to all His indwelling, to obey the injunction, and "have the mind of Christ."

THE LIFE OF THE CHRISTIAN—ITS TESTING.

" Gold is not hurt by the fire. The stone is not marred by the sculptor's hewing. 'While the marble wastes the image grows.' At the last that which will be most beautiful in us will not be what we have saved from the hammer, but the marks which will tell of the deepest cuttings of the chisel."—J. R. Miller, "The Making of Character."

"Let thy gold be cast in the furnace,
   Thy red gold, precious and bright,
Do not fear the hungry fire,
   With its caverns of burning light:
And thy gold shall return more precious,
   Free from every spot and stain;
For gold must be tried by fire,
   As a heart must be tried by pain!

In the cruel fire of Sorrow
   Cast thy heart, do not faint or wail;
Let thy hand be firm and steady,
   Do not let thy spirit quail:
But wait till the trial is over,
   And take thy heart again;
For as gold is tried by fire,
   So a heart must be tried by pain!

I shall know by the gleam and glitter
   Of the golden chain you wear,
By your heart's calm strength in loving,
   Of the fire they have had to bear.
Beat on, true heart, forever;
   Shine bright, strong golden chain;
And bless the cleansing fire,
   And the furnace of living pain!"
—A. A. Procter.

CHAPTER V.

THE LIFE OF THE CHRISTIAN—ITS TESTING.

"And bring us not into temptation, but deliver us from the evil." Matt. vi. 13.

"Wherefore let him that thinketh he standeth take heed lest he fall. There hath no temptation taken you but such as man can bear: but God is faithful, Who will not suffer you to be tempted above that ye are able, but will with the temptation make also the way of escape, that ye may be able to endure it." I. Cor. x. 12-13.

"Count it all joy, my brethren, when ye fall into manifold temptations; knowing that the proving of your faith worketh patience. And let patience have its perfect work, that ye may be perfect and entire, lacking in nothing." James i. 2-4.

In approaching the subject of the testing of the Christian life I want to speak of the purpose and process thereof.

The present life of the Christian is preparatory and progressive. Nothing is more evident in a study of the New Testament than that the people of God are finally a heavenly people. I do not mean by that they are indifferent to the present world, or that they are to live the life of a physical separation from it, or shut themselves within walls to escape it. But the fact remains that the Christian life, as to its ultimate purpose, can never be perfected in this life. This is our school time. We are in training. We are growing and developing towards maturity of life, in order to the perfect service of the ages to come. Our true service will commence when this probationary life is past, and the life of heaven has begun. Paul, in his letter to the Ephesians, reveals the vocation of the Church to be heavenly in its nature. In the ages to come in union with Christ, she will witness to principalities and powers in the heavenlies of God's wondrous grace and wisdom.

Of course, while all this is true, the Church has a present service and responsibility, and it must never be forgotten that we are saved to serve even here and now. The communication of the life of Christ to the soul is not merely for personal salvation, but in order that through the saved, Christ may carry forward His great work of saving others. Our present work is that of showing forth the excellencies of God, and so revealing to men the perfection of His government. It is only as our hearts are set upon the heavenly calling, that we shall be able to fulfill the earthly calling. It is only as the radiant vision of the vocation to come is before us, that we shall be able to fulfill the vocation of the shadows and the mists and the mysteries of the little while. Each one of us is called to some specific work. Not all are called to the work of preaching or teaching, but all are responsible concerning this ministry of revelation. These two facts concerning service must be remembered. The Church is created supremely for service hereafter. There is also a service here, partial, incomplete, and transitory, yet important and glorious. All the present, however, is but preparatory to the future, and temptation means the testing of those who are being prepared for service, as to their fitness for their work. All through the process of present service temptation will be the portion of the Christian. All through these days of discipline and preparation for the final service, testing will be necessary.

The word temptation is often misunderstood, being used as if it meant only seduction toward evil, whereas that is a process of temptation. Temptation is not allurement toward evil necessarily. Allurement toward evil is a method of temptation. "Count it all joy, my brethren, when ye fall into manifold temptations," and no inspired apostle would charge us to count it all joy when we find ourselves in the presence of evil, and feel the pull of its allurement. But the purpose of the testing or temptation was in the mind of James when he wrote those words. The purpose of testing or temptation was also in the mind of Paul when he wrote to the Corinthian Christians, "There hath no temptation taken you but such as man can bear: but God is faithful, Who will not suffer you to be tempted above that ye are able, but will with the temptation make also the way of escape." In the New Testament where this word is made use of, while it is used to describe the alluring of the soul by evil, it nevertheless always indicates the fact that by such allurement the work of testing is going forward. This testing may come in other ways, and that is why I have chosen to speak of testing, rather than temptation. I want to make two propositions and consider them each a little. The first is that testing to the Christian is always in the line of, and with a view to preparation for service. The second proposition is that the whole process of testing is under the direct supervision of God.

Testing is always necessary as part of preparation for service. It reveals the strength or weakness of the life at any given moment, and thus creates confidence, or calls for increasing carefulness and reinforcement at some point of weakness. If in the process of testing I am victorious, then my strength is thereby revealed, and I am prepared for some new lesson, or some new service. If under testing I fail, then my weakness is revealed, and I am driven back to Christ in order that there may be the strengthening of that in me which is weak, and the putting away of that which caused the failure. While it is true that we do fall under temptation, it is also true that there is no necessity for any such falling. If such a statement is startling, let us remember the words "God will not suffer you to be tempted above that ye are able." It will be objected that being tempted we fall before we are aware of it, but that there is no necessity for any such defeat is evident from the words "Who will not suffer you to be tempted above that ye are able, but will with the temptation make also the way of escape."

If under temptation I fall, what has temptation done for me? It has revealed a point of weakness, and such revelation should drive me back again to Christ, in order that alone with Him I may first make confession of my sin and failure, and then in order that I may anew take hold upon His strength at the point of weakness, and be no more overcome. So that in the life of the Christian, testing has always a blessing associated with it. "Count it all joy, my brethren, when ye fall into manifold temptations."

Yet Christ commanded us "Pray, that ye enter not into temptation," and thereby defined the true attitude of the soul toward testing. Of this, however, more presently. To return to the subject of the value of testing.

"Count it all joy, my brethren, when ye fall into manifold temptations," and why? Because "the proving or testing of your faith worketh steadfastness." Testing ever issues in blessing to such as abide loyal to Christ. If victorious over it, it has revealed strength which proves readiness for fuller service and larger life. If defeated, it has revealed a weakness, and if the revelation of that weakness does but drive us to Christ, in order that we may take hold anew upon His strength, then even the testing has proved a blessing.

We must be careful to differentiate between temptation and sin. Temptation is in itself a veritable means of grace if only it drive us to Christ. In that way in the largest and fullest sense, we may rise on our dead selves to higher things. A bridge is tested as to its power to carry weight, because the work of the bridge will be that of carrying weight. Metal is tested as to its resistance, because the work of the metal will be to resist. That is ever the true law of testing. It always tries the quality of something which is necessary to the fulfillment of purpose. There are many methods but the purpose is always the same. Just as a bridge is tested as to its ability to bear weight, because its work is to bear weight; and just as metal is tested as to its power of resistance, because its work is to be that of resistance; so the Christian is tested as to his capacity for that particular form of service to which he is called.

Let us see how this applies to the Christian Church. Take the whole outlook upon the Christian Church, not in its final vocation but in its present work and service. The apostle said, "Ye are . . . that ye may show forth the excellencies of Him Who called you out of darkness into His marvellous light." Never was anything more wonderful said of the Church than that. She is God's medium for the manifestation of Himself to the world, the instrument through which the illumination of His own nature and character shall shine upon the ways of men, the vehicle in which the vision of God shall be conveyed to men. The testings of the Church therefore from the world, the flesh, and the devil, are directed toward her essential function of the manifestation of God, her fitness for the realization and revelation of His excellencies. It is in the realm of her fitness for the fulfillment of that function, that testing ever comes, not to hinder her, but to prove capacity. We saw in the previous study that the relation of the Christian to God as revealed in Jesus Christ was characterized by confidence, by communion, and by coöperation. The Church of Jesus Christ will manifest the excellencies of God in proportion as she is living the life of confidence in God, the life of communion with God, and the life of coöperation with God. We are to express the truth concerning God to men, to the angels, to the ages. This we are able to do in proportion as our confidence in God is complete, our communion is constant, and our coöperation is consecrated. Within the compass of these facts, therefore, of confidence, of communion, and coöperation, all our testing will come. Such testing of the Church's confidence has come in times of persecution, in baptisms of blood. In periods of fiery persecution the Church was being tested as to her confidence in God, and if such testing sometimes revealed lack of confidence and she fell back, yet more often it manifested the strength of confidence, and made her more strong, so that the testimony of the Church to the world was stronger and purer in those days than in the times when testing was lacking.

The testing of the Church will come along the line of her communion with God. That is one of the peculiar perils of the present age. The devil of the medieval ages has passed away as to his methods of manifestation, but he is still with us. One of his methods today is starting so many organizations, that the church members have no time for communion with God. The Church is so busy that one cannot move without hearing the clink and the friction of her wheels. Whenever the Church becomes so fussy about her work, that she has no time for communion with God, the world looks on, and smiles at her, and helps her in her bazaars, and stays away from her prayer-meetings. Oh that God would turn us back to communion with Himself! Oh that we might turn back in these days to the quiet meditation of those past days! Oh that we might make time to sit at His feet! The trouble is that we have yielded to the spirit of the age so largely. Wherever you find a church or a people who will make time for communion, notwithstanding the rush of life, there is the church that is strong. I care nothing for numbers or finances. It is only in communion that there can be the fulfillment of service.

So also the testing of the Church will come along the line of her coöperation with God. In proportion as the Church is in fellowship with the Lord Jesus Christ, counting that her chief business, coöperating with God in the midst of every passing age, in that proportion she is fulfilling the purpose of God. But when the Church is trying to catch the spirit of the age, and accommodate herself to the movements of the age, and express all the great doctrines in the terms of the time, she is missing the mark, she will not exert her influence.

This is the broader outlook. To come now from the general to the particular, and to speak of individual testing—and this still in the realm of service—let us suppose that God is calling to some place of conspicuous service, some position seen and beheld of men, and talked of by the world. In that place of conspicuous service the real responsibility of the saint is that of revealing God. Whether the call be to the work of the prophet, evangelist, teacher, or to testimony in the circle of society in which we move, or in our business relationships, our true work is ever that of Divine revelation. For any such service there are two qualities necessary, courage and humility; daring to come to the front if God calls, accompanied by that humility of spirit which ever recognizes the Lordship of Christ over all His servants, and therefore is free from boasting.

It is in the matter of these essential qualities that testing will come to the man or woman called to the place of conspicuous service. It matters nothing as to the argument, who the agent of temptation may be, or along what particular avenue the temptation may come, the qualities tested will be the same. The greatest perils of such responsibility are cowardice and pride. Moses was tested in the matter of courage when he asked God "Who am I;" and for the moment was in danger of allowing his own incompetence to eclipse the vision of the ability of God. Many have failed because they have not dared to enter on some path of service clearly marked out for them. There is a false modesty which is cowardice.

Take a case now exactly opposite. God may have called

ITS TESTING

me into some place of hidden service. The qualities necessary for success are fidelity and contentment; fidelity, the determination to obey, because God has called, even though no one should criticize or commend, no one help or hinder. The temptation often comes in the form of restlessness, and the desire to do some greater thing. It will suggest the meanness of the task to be done, proposing a change in the life. This will tend to break down fidelity, and make me discontented in the place where God has put me. As capacity for service is the highest fact in Christian life, testing is all-important, as it reveals the weakness or manifests the strength of the instrument.

Now let us approach the second proposition, that the process of testing is under the direction and supervision of God. The book of Job is the supreme book of the Bible illustrating this truth. Satan could not touch a single hair upon the back of a single camel that belonged to Job until he had been and asked leave of God. We have some strange ideas about the devil. We seem to think he is running loose, and doing all he wants to do. If you are not submitted to God then it is no use resisting the devil, for he is hoodwinking you, and leading you where he wants you to go. But if you are submitted to God, then God holds the reins of the chargers upon which the devil rides, and He "will not suffer you to be tested beyond that which you are able." He will not allow any pressure to be brought against us greater than we have strength at the moment to resist, and with the temptation He will open the door of escape. He will not suffer us to be tested beyond the breaking point. This is a great announcement. The agents of temptation, Satan, the circumstances of life, and the frailty of the flesh, are all known and watched, and held in check by God Himself. The world, the flesh, and the devil, these are the agents of temptation, and none of them will be permitted to bring to bear upon the life of the believer greater pressure than that life is able to bear. He will permit them to try us up to a certain point, and we never need break down, for the door of escape is always provided when the limit of our ability is reached; and we may pass out from the process triumphant.

"Simon, Simon, behold, Satan asked to have you that he might sift you as wheat." Notice carefully that he was compelled to ask. He could not put these men through the process of sifting save under Divine permission. And yet even more carefully notice what follows, "But I made supplication for thee," that is the provision of the door of escape. And that supplication of love prevailed. The faith of these men never failed, nor did their love, even though their courage did. Faith is confidence in a person, and if in these men, that failed in any respect, it was only their confidence in His ability to do what they thought He was about to do. Their faith never failed in Christ Himself. The two men walking to Emmaus, speaking of Him called Him "a Prophet mighty in deed and word." Their hope failed, and their confidence in His success, but not their faith in Himself. And men are not saved by believing anything about Jesus, but by belief in Him.

We cannot be tested without the knowledge and watchfulness of God. Just as the refiner of silver sits in the presence of the furnace, and with skilled eye watches until the fire has done its work, and then withdraws the precious metal; so God, in infinite care for His own, governs the heat, and the measure of the fire; and will not suffer any to be tempted above that they are able to bear.

This is equally true with regard to circumstances, or the world. How often we affirm that circumstances are too strong for us. That is never true. God is always mightier than the circumstances, and all the world forces which pull us downward, are also under His control. If we live in right relationship to Him, then we are mightier than all the forces of the world. "Greater is He that is in you, than he that is in the world." John is speaking there of antichrist, not as a person manifested, but as a spirit and influence. True it is that the spirit of the world is mighty, but that in us which pulls as against the world is mightier still. Consequently while we are allowed to feel the attractiveness of the world for the testing of our life, God knows, watches, and holds in check these subtle forces; but by the Spirit He in us is mightier than the world, as He is stronger than Satan.

So also with the flesh. In the natural life there are appetites which in themselves are perfectly right, but which tend to lead astray by seducing us from the realm of law for their satisfaction. The lust of them, the desire of the flesh, pulls us from the path of rectitude and loyalty. This also He knows, and limits; and the lust of the Spirit is mightier than the lust of the flesh.

Yet there must be this testing of the lust of the flesh, in order that we may know the might of the lust of the Spirit. There must be the testing of the pride of the world, in order that we may know the might of His power. There must be the testing of the adversary in order that we may know the strength of Him Who is mightier than the foe. Life lived in Him is tested by all these forces, but is victorious over them.

Not only the agents of temptation, but the avenues also, natural desire, spiritual aspiration, and vocational ambition are all under His control. The only avenues along which the adversary can reach a human soul are these. He exhausted his methods in the wilderness. He approached Jesus first along the line of natural desire as to His hunger; and then through spiritual aspiration as to His trust in God; and finally as to His vocational ambition, in the offer of the kingdoms. The final thing in every life is what it has to do. We are, in order that we may do.

First then, the natural desires of the physical, which is the lower part of nature, will be tempted. Secondly, the spiritual aspirations. Lastly, the vocational ambitions. The devil has nothing beyond these. He has a thousand baits, but only three avenues of approach. These are all under the control of God. Though all must feel the force of testing, He knows the strength, and is conscious of the weakest moment, and accordingly He limits the forces of temptation, and opens the door of escape. Satan can never sift without permission granted. The world or circumstances may seem too powerful, but He will act against them in our weakest moment. The flesh may seem to be wholly on the side of the foe, yet He is able to quicken even the mortal body.

The life in us now being tested is the Christ life. We are Christians because that life is in us. Of that life Christ is Himself the sustenance. The outward expression of the life is Christ, just as its consciousness is His.

So the testing of the Christian life is the testing of the Christ life in us. That life has already had its perfect victory. Therefore if we meet the testing of the enemy in its strength, we meet it in the power of a victory already gained. Testing in that energy always issues in triumph.

Many fall under testing. This is always because the laws of the Christ life are not obeyed. This may be proved by going back honestly to the point of failure. Let any such defeat be remembered, and the question asked concerning it. Need I have fallen there if I had absolutely depended upon Jesus Christ? There is not one of us who dare say Yes. We all fall, but always because we did not look for the door of escape, or else did not meet the testing in His strength alone. Failure often comes because we do not remember the spirit and meaning of that petition which our Lord taught us to offer, "Lead us not into temptation, but deliver us from the evil." The principal matter is that we should be delivered from evil. If the final purity cannot be attained save by the way of testing, then we must consent to pass through it. Testing should always be approached with that cautiousness of spirit which results from the consciousness of its peril, and yet with confidence that He will finally deliver us from evil.

In brief, as Christ has given us life, and is able to sustain that life, so also is He able to make us victorious, "more than conquerors" over all the forces that are against us; and when we depend on Him in testing, whether it be through Satan, the world, or the flesh, then testing itself becomes a means of grace, a fiery process through which the dross is burned, and the gold made to shine perfectly.

THE LIFE OF THE CHRISTIAN—ITS VALUE.

"From the brightness of the glory,
   Go ye forth," He said;
"Heal the sick and cleanse the lepers,
   Raise the dead.
Freely give I thee the treasure,
   Freely give the same;
Take no store of gold or silver—
   Take My Name.

* * * *

"Thou shalt tell Me in the glory
   All that thou hast done,
Setting forth alone; returning
   Not alone.
Thou shalt bring the ransomed with thee,
   They with songs shall come
As the golden sheaves of harvest,
   Gathered home."

* * * * * *

"Thus with instruments of music
   Do His servants stand
Harp and lute the King has fashioned
   With His hand.
And 'the music of Jehovah'
   Sounds from every chord;
He who makes that glorious music
   Is the Lord.

"He by them tells forth God's praises
   To the ears of men,
And to God His praise ascendeth
   Yet again.
He alone, the Mighty Preacher,
   Gathering in His own,
And the praise to God returning,
   His alone."

      —T. P.
"Hymns of Ter Steegen, Suso and Others."

CHAPTER VI.

THE LIFE OF THE CHRISTIAN—ITS VALUE.

"And He said unto them, It is not for you to know times or seasons, which the Father hath set within His own authority. But ye shall receive power, when the Holy Spirit is come upon you: and ye shall be My witnesses both in Jerusalem, and in all Judæa and Samaria, and unto the uttermost part of the earth." Acts i. 7-8.

"So then, my beloved, even as ye have always obeyed, not as in my presence only, but now much more in my absence, work out your own salvation with fear and trembling; for it is God Who worketh in you both to will and to work, for His good pleasure. Do all things without murmurings and questionings; that ye may become blameless and harmless, children of God without blemish in the midst of a crooked and perverse generation, among whom ye are seen as lights in the world, holding forth the word of life." Phil. ii. 12-16.

Of all the facts concerning the Divine method in creation, none is more perpetually evident, or needs more constant enforcement than that of purpose lying within potentiality. In other words, no creation of God fulfills its highest exercise of being, save in relation to existences other than its own. No creation of God is self-centred and self-sufficient. Of God alone can these conditions of being be affirmed. Everything which He has created, from a flower to an archangel is created for a purpose. Each flower fulfills a ministry in the very fact of its blossoming, and every angel is a flame of fire for the purpose of ministry. When man perfectly understands creation he will clearly see that the most insignificant and apparently useless forms of life have some part to play in the great economy of God. The Divine ideal of humanity is that of its solidarity, and although through sin, factions and strifes have destroyed the ideal, yet the proportion in the passing of the centuries in which man has secured his own well-being is the proportion in which he has learned the relationship of each to all, and the contribution of all to each. Power for the fulfillment of the purpose of the thing created, always lies within it. It is invariably possible for every work of God to fulfill the purpose of its being. These principles obtain in the spiritual realm as certainly as in every other. Christ did not come to destroy or set aside any principle of Divine creation, or of government, but to recognize and realize. Every Christian, therefore, has a value in his day and generation, and the proportion in which the life of Christ is reproduced in the individual is the proportion in which that value is realized. As we have seen, the Christian is one sharing the life of Christ. That life being diligently sustained, and clearly expressed, it will fulfill definite functions.

In the commencement of the Colossian epistle which deals principally with the glory of Christ, the apostle referring to creation declares that "He is the Firstborn of all creation," and dealing with His relation to the Church, he speaks of Him as the "Firstborn from the dead." Of the wonderful realm which we call Nature, Christ is the Firstborn. He is the Origin of all the varied forms of beauty with which we are familiar in Nature. It is in

Him that they consist, or hold together. It is moreover, for Him they were and have been created. Thus the great principle of purpose within potentiality manifest in Nature, is directly related to the originating and sustaining Christ.

In the realm of the new creation He is Firstborn from the dead. So that here also the truth of purpose and of power is immediately related to Him. The new life of the Christian is life which He won out of death. As in every flower related to Him there is a purpose fulfilled in its blossoming, so in every new-born life related to Him as life out of death, there is a purpose to be fulfilled, and power equal to its fulfillment. We are not simply saved that we may be saved. We are saved rather that we may serve. Thus in every soul Christ-indwelt and governed, there is that which is of value to God Himself.

In the Ephesian epistle, which is the complement to that to the Colossian, we find the remarkable declaration that God has an inheritance in His people, that is, that God gains something in His people. A study of the whole context will show that He gains nothing of glory, nothing of enrichment, but a medium through which He is able to manifest His glory, and show forth the riches of His grace. While the great fulfillment of its purpose will never be realized until the Church is perfected in its union with Christ in the ages to come, it is nevertheless true that in measure the principle is fulfilled even here and now in every Christian soul. The very fact of living the Christ life does in itself fulfill a purpose, and in all such living there is value in the economy of God. In the truest and deepest sense of the word, Christian service is not something externally added to Christian life. It is a service rendered in the very act of life. Each Christian by being a Christian in all the full sense of the word, is exerting the power of God for the accomplishment of His purpose. It is the value of such living that we are now to consider. Given the life whose nature is Christ, whose sustenance is Christ, whose expression is Christ, whose consciousness is Christ, and whose testing is the testing of the Christ life, such life has a definite present value in the world. The value is threefold, and may broadly be described as that of testimony, of activity, and of vindication.

The life of the Christian is a perpetual testimony in the world to certain great truths. It is moreover an unceasing coöperation with God; and finally it is, through such testimony and such coöperation, a vindication of God in the midst of godlessness.

The Christian life is first a testimony to the reality of spiritual things. It will at once be seen how close a connection there is between this thought and that of the consciousness of the Christian dealt with previously. That consciousness is of God, and of eternity, the overwhelming certainty in the life of the reality of the things unseen, eternal, and spiritual. A Christian soul, sharing Christ's consciousness, believes far more in God Who is unseen, than in anything which can be seen; is far more certain of the infinite unseen, than of the finite seen. A Christian is more sure of God than of men, of eternity than of time, of the spiritual than of the material. All this is, of course, diametrically opposed to the consciousness of a man of the world. He is not sure of God, is indeed, an agnostic, yet imagines himself to be perfectly sure of man. He is not sure of eternity, but feels quite sure of time. He is by no means convinced of the reality of spiritual things, but is sure of things material. This contrast at once reveals the fact of testimony. The life of the Christian is a witness amid material things to the reality of the spiritual. I do not here merely mean that the Christian in speech will refer to God, to heaven, to spiritual things. All that he will assuredly do, but testimony in speech is of no avail save as the life of the one who speaks is being lived in actual relation to the things of which he speaks. It is this life of conscious relationship which is the most powerful testimony to the reality of these things. The essential greatness of the Puritans was that of their recognition of the spiritual realm, and of the eternities. They had their roughnesses, which after all, were but the excrescences of greatness, but they were men whose lives were centred in God, and circumferenced by the spiritual. Yet they were no dreamers, having lost their consciousness of, and sympathy with, the actualities of the passing day. As we look back on them through the centuries they are seen as giants, whose feet were firmly planted upon the earth, but whose heads ever seemed lifted into the heavenly spaces. They acted, they suffered, they even fought, but behind everything, as impulse of all, was a consciousness of God, and the value of spiritual things. Notwithstanding all the limitations of their age, they were such men as broke down tyrannies, emancipated peoples, and laid broad and strong the foundations of new nations. They did not retire from the midst of the corruption of the world, and give themselves to ascetic practices. They rather laid violent hands upon the world, wrestled with its problems, combatted its corruptions, and breathed into it the very spirit of life. Believing in God, they talked of Him, and toiled for Him. Having seen the vision of "the city that hath the foundations, whose builder and maker is God," through strain and stress and storm, they wrought toward the establishment upon this earth of conditions corresponding thereto. How well they wrought the centuries have told. Let their children ever be careful that on such foundations they build not hay, and wood, and stubble; but gold, silver, and precious stones.

Every devout Christian is in these deeper senses of the word, a Puritan, not perhaps resembling them in some of the accidental peculiarities of their age, but in essential testimony borne to the reality of the eternal, the unseen, the spiritual. A Christian then is one who lives among men, prosecuting his ordinary business, or professional avocation within the spaciousness of spiritual sight. A Christian will take hold of every duty, and fulfill it, recognizing its relation to an infinite order. In the simplest matters this will be true. In the selection of a dwelling place the infinite will never be lost sight of. Alas that this should so often be forgotten, and that by those professing to be Christians. In the choice of a house the principle of selection is so constantly material. The locality, the climate, the class of people dwelling in the neighbourhood, and so seldom the spiritual, the nearness of the sanctuary, the character of the ministry, the opportunity for the cultivation of the highest life of the children. This is not Christianity, it is rather civilized paganism. The true Christian will never forget the matter of supreme importance. The Christian youth will face life, asking the same question that all will ask, and yet with a different relation, and sense of values. What am I going to do with my life? is the question of all young people sooner or later. But the Christian will say, What am I going to do with my life in the light of eternity? How can I make the most of it for God? That is the true principle of selection. It is not unnatural, nor is it strained. To those who judge only by material standards it may seem a strange and unnecessary question. It is the natural principle of selection to the truly Christ-filled soul. The home, the calling in life, the recreation, everything in short, is to be decided upon, and held in relation to infinite values and realities. Nothing is judged in the light of today, but all in the light of the ages to come. The Christian stands forever, not in the circumscribed circle of the passing hour, but in the infinite circle of the eternal life. All such as live in this conscious and manifest relation to the spiritual and unseen will bear testimony to the reality of the spiritual; and, indeed, will do more to convince the world of that reality than all philosophic arguments.

The value of the life of the Christian to God then is first of all its testimony to the actuality and supremacy of spiritual things.

And yet the Christian life bears other testimony. It is a constant witness to the possibility of victory over all the evil in the midst of which life has to be lived. There are two phrases which are commonly heard on the lips of men of the world, but which can never be heard by those who are living fully consecrated Christian lives, save perchance in order that their inference may be denied. Men may constantly be heard speaking of "necessary evils," and declaring that "of two evils we must choose the less." The life of the Christian denies the claims of both these phrases. There is no such thing as a "necessary evil." The conjunction of the words creates a contradiction of terms. If evil, then not necessary. If necessary, then not evil. Nothing that is really necessary can be evil. Nothing that is surely evil can be necessary. A Christian will say, Of two evils I decline to choose either. It is a favourite device of the enemy to suggest that sometimes only two paths stretch out before the Christian, treading either of which he must be guilty of some declination from the line of rectitude. The true Christian indwelt by the Christ will bear the testimony of the Christ, and that is, that evil never need be chosen. There is always a third alternative. Let a superlative illustration help us at this point. It is often urged that men come to occasions where there is no escape from wrong doing in greater or less degree. Many years ago, before the Christian Mission had become the Salvation Army, and before its evangelists became officers, wearing uniforms, William Booth was one day travelling in a railway carriage, when three men stepped in at a wayside station, and as the train proceeded, engaged in conversation concerning the fact that they had procured for certain premises a license for the sale of strong drink. They spoke of the advantages of the situation, and of the great success that was assured to them in the conduct of the business. William Booth sat and listened until his soul burned within him, and then turning to them, he told them that he had listened to their conversation with interest, that he had heard all they had said about the advantages of the property and the certainty of great financial success. But, he continued, that there were things of which he had not heard them say one word, that would invariably be connected with the conduct of their business. He told them they had said nothing about ruined homes and broken hearts and degraded womanhood and blighted children and damned souls. "All these things, gentlemen," said he, "will result from your successful business." Of course, an argument ensued, until at last one man, feeling the force of the passionate words of the earnest man, said in self-defence, "But, Sir, I must live, and I have no other means of livelihood." The reply of the Christian came clear and sharp, "My dear sir, there is no necessity that you should live at all. The one thing necessary is that you should be pure, and if to keep your purity you must die, then you had better die." That is undoubtedly a superlative illustration, and yet it is a true illustration of the Christian's attitude toward evil. Evil is never necessary, and under no circumstances need it be chosen. Sin is utterly useless to men for the fulfillment of the highest possibilities of their lives, and consequently is always unnecessary. There can come no occasion when it is needful to choose even what may be spoken of as a "less evil!" Death is for ever preferable to wrongdoing. That is surely the meaning of the whole story of the martyrs and confessors of the past, and surely also it is the testimony that Christians should constantly bear in the present age, and, indeed, the testimony which they must bear, if in them and through them Christ lives and works.

The value of the life of the Christian is that it, and it alone, bears unequivocal and uncompromising testimony against sin. The philosophy of the age which is not Christian, is inclined to condone and account for sin, speaking of it as temperamental, a process of evolution, a continuous abnormality, affirming that the degree or nature of sin depends upon the colour of a man's hair, or the shape of his head. A Christian life makes no such compromise. It declares that sin is devilish, and damnable. It stands erect and protests that death is for ever preferable to sin in any shape.

To bring this to a more particular and personal application for a moment, the Christian life bears testimony to the possibility of victory over evil within the nature. When the man of the world declares that righteousness and purity are impossible to him, because of the fires of lust and passion which lie within the very fibre of his being, the Christian will answer, Such fires burned within me also, but "where sin abounded, grace did abound more exceedingly." The fires are quenched, the chain is broken, and I have been made free from the law of sin and death in the victorious energy of the Spirit of life. The thing I could not, now I can. The thing I was compelled to do, which yet I hated, now I am enabled to do no longer. I who once was the slave of passion am now master of passion in the principle and power of the Christ life. How great and gracious is the value of such testimony in the midst of sense and sin-bound men and women.

And yet once again, the Christian life bears testimony to the true balance of human nature, the inter-relationship of all the sides of complex personality. Christian life is a revelation of the fact that all that God gives a man in the first creation is realized in the new birth. Everything that the Christian is by the creation of God in his natural life, he will continue to be by the new creation of Christ through the Spirit. All men are born into the world with fires and forces slumbering within them, for the presence of which God is not responsible. These will be quenched and broken by the incoming of the Christ life, in order that the true man, according to the Divine intention may find himself, and be manifested to the world. Thus it may be repeated that everything that God created in individual life is realized and crowned in the life of the Christian.

All intellectual capacities will expand and grow in Christian life. All artistic possibilities will find fullest and most glorious means of manifestation where the life is truly Christian. Has God bestowed that mystic acuteness of hearing which becomes conscious of symphonies that ordinary mortals never heard? Christ will not spoil the music, but make possible its expression. In the first creation has God bestowed that quality of vision which takes in the landscape's sweep, and holds in view all its delicacy of colour? Christ will not spoil the picture. He will rather free the life from such fires of passion, as being allowed to burn will befog and spoil the glorious vision. The Christian is one in whom all the life God created is delivered from the forces that spoil, and all its parts are brought into such coöperative unity that it shall bear testimony to the perfection of the Divine ideal. The life of the Christian, therefore, testifies not merely to the reality of spiritual things, but to the influence of such things upon the material forces, and their power to ennoble and crown every side of life.

It may now be stated that the value of Christian life through such testimony is that of positive activity. To live thus is to cooperate with God. All Christian living is a contribution to the well-being of the state, to the forces making for righteousness and love as the regnant qualities in human life, and so toward the sum total of God's final victory. Men do not always recognize the value of Christian life to the well-being of the state, though it is indeed great. Imagine for one single moment what would be the issue if all Christian people were taken out of London, New York, or any of our cities, or from the nations of the world. Surely the Master understood perfectly the true value of His own teaching when obeyed in the lives of men; and He said to the little band of disciples, who, submissive to His authority, were realizing His purposes, "Ye are the salt of the earth . . . ye are the light of the world." Every Christian life is of the nature of salt, antispetic, purifying, preventing the spread of corruption. Every Christian life is light, shining in a dark place, and the whole company of the Church in the world at any given moment creates a light that men most need in the darkness of sorrow and of sin. Salt never forms an association to purify anything, but it purifies everything, and this simply by being salt. The light beams never form a society of any kind, but they illuminate, and this simply by shining. The Christian life is salt, and therefore it purifies. It is light and therefore it illuminates. All Christians are not called to preach, nor even to teach, nor yet to hold official positions within the Church, but all are called to live. The life of the Christian must prevent impurity. If you are indeed a Christian, then when you enter the room some kinds of conversation must cease, not because it is expected you will rebuke it in words even if you heard it, but because of what you are. That is a simple illustration of the great principle. The Christian life is light moreover, falling everywhere upon the darkness, revealing it, and yet revealing it only as it passes, dissipated by the shining. It is in the shining of the light that the great work is accomplished. Occasions will arise where sin must be rebuked by actual speech, but the forcefulness of the rebuke will be created by the shining of the life. Occasions will arise where tender words of sympathy will be spoken to the soul distressed, and yet the words will come as balm in proportion to the shining of the quiet life, or of the life itself comforted with the comfort of God.

George Campbell, one of the sweetest of Christian men, who devoted his life very largely to the work of temperance reform, once administered a rebuke on a public platform of the severest kind. An avowed atheist who had spoken before him in the interests of temperance, appealed to the strength of human will for the overcoming of the appetite for drink, and referring to the uselessness of any aid outside a man's will. In a contemptuous aside he said, "The man who invented gas has done more for the human race than all the preachers of Christianity." When George Campbell rose to address the meeting he began by saying, "I have been interested to hear my friend's opinion of what benefits humanity. If tomorrow I should be plunged in sorrow, or should find myself approaching the end of this brief life, I should desire some preacher of the Cross to tell me again its story for my comfort and my strength. I presume that my friend under similar circumstances would send for the gasfitter!" The rebuke was sharp, and severe, but the power of it to the audience who heard it was created by what they knew of the character of George Campbell. His life was salt, and his speech, therefore, seasoned with it, was antiseptic. His life was light, and his words also were spirit and life.

Thus it is true that the Christian life is one of coöperative activity with God. Every Christian life is a contribution to the force that makes for righteousness and makes for love; and wherever man, woman, or child lives in true relation to Christ, there is being exerted by such life a part of that mighty energy of God in Christ, whereby at last He will heal all wounds, and dry all tears, and build the city for which men have looked through long centuries, the city in which there shall be no evil thing.

And yet once more. The Christian life is a vindication of God in the midst of a skeptical and unbelieving age. Men standing outside the realm of personal loyalty to Him, can never understand His method because they do not understand His purpose. The result is ever that of criticism and opposition. "The mind of the flesh is enmity against God." It questions the wisdom of His action because it does not know the reason thereof. The Christian knows God's purpose, and therefore trusts His method. I do not say that the method is always understood, but by the Christian soul it is resolutely set in the light of the sure purpose of God, which is our perfecting. Then through the method of the fire, and of the testing, and of the discipline the Christian passes with songs of triumph and of testimony, and so God is vindicated in the face of the criticism and the unbelief of the age. Christian men and women in conduct issuing from character, both of which are admirable in the eyes of the world, vindicate the method of God as they contribute to the understanding of His purpose. In them His thought is seen to be a hedge of love; and the fires of testing and of trial are revealed as gracious messengers which never burn the pure gold, but destroy only the dross. Thus a Christian, who, in the midst of suffering is patient and full of a quiet peace and joy, is vindicating God against all the criticism of half-blind philosophy.

In this fact there is at least a partial solution of the mystery of the suffering of the saints. When the morning dawns, and the mists have rolled from the valleys, and life is seen in the light of the eternal purpose and counsel, then it will be known that suffering was often highest service; and that passing along the pathway of pain, while yet maintaining a quiet trust, the life was preaching of God to an unbelieving age in a way more powerful than any possible save to such suffering.

It is impossible to live the life of quiet calm trust in God in the midst of the turmoil and unrest of this feverish age without creating an atmosphere of quietness and peace of which all will become conscious. The atmosphere is a vindication of God, for it results from trust implicitly reposed in Him. We have never looked upon the courageous confidence of some sorrowing saint who through all the painful process has evidenced a quiet strength and a great heart satisfaction, without having realized that God's methods were vindicated in His children.

For these purposes Christians exist. The value of every Christian life is that of positive and powerful testimony to the reality of the spiritual, the possibility of victory over evil, and the beauty of the Divine ideal in human life. This testimony is in itself of the nature of powerful fellowship in activity with God.

And finally wherever the Christian life is clearly seen, it becomes an argument vindicating God against all the criticisms of unbelief. Christianity is infinitely more than the salvation of the individual. It is that, but with the larger purpose of creating an influence, exerting an opinion, and encompassing an end. The goal toward which Christ moved was the setting up of the Kingship of God, and the restoration of a lost order. All such as share His life have that same goal in view. The whole creation groans in its limitation, and waits for the manifestation of the sons of God. Every such present manifestation is a contribution to the breaking of humanity's bonds, the ending of the race's limitation, and the changing of groaning into acclamation and worship.

By Rev. F. B. Meyer

The Shepherd Psalm. Illustrated. Printed in two colors. 12mo, cloth, gilt top, boxed, $1.25; full gilt, $1.50.

The Bells of Is. Echoes from my early pastorates. With portrait. 12mo, cloth, 75 c.

Prayers for Heart and Home. 8vo, flex. cloth, 75 c.

Paul: a Servant of Jesus Christ. 12mo, cloth, $1.00.

Old Testament Heroes. 8 vols., 12mo, cloth, each, $1.00; the set, boxed, $8.00.

    Abraham.   Elijah.   Jeremiah.   Joshua.
    David.   Israel.   Joseph.   Moses.

The Expository Series. 12mo, cloth, each $1.00; the set, boxed, $4.00.

    Tried by Fire.   The Way Into the Holiest.
    Christ in Isaiah.   The Life and Light of Men.

The Christian Life Series. 18mo, cloth, each, 30 c.

    The Shepherd Psalm   Through Fire and Flood.
    Christian Living.   The Glorious Lord.
    The Present Tenses   Calvary to Pentecost.
    The Future Tenses   Key Words to the Inner Life.

    ₄ The first four also issued in flexible, decorated cloth, 16mo, each, 50 c.; the set, boxed, $2.00.

Addresses. 12mo, paper, each, 15 c.; cloth, each, net, 30 c.

    Meet for the Master's Use   A Castaway
    The Secret of Guidance   Light on Life's Duties

Saved and Kept. Long 16mo, cloth, 50 c.

Cheer for Life's Pilgrimage. Long 16mo, cloth, 50 c.

Peace, Perfect Peace. 18mo, cloth, 25 c.

The Psalms. Notes and Readings. 18mo, cloth, 60 c.

Envelope Series of Booklets. Packets Nos. 1 and 2, each containing 12 Tracts, assorted, net, 20 c.

Choice Extracts. 24mo, paper, each, 5 c.; per doz. net, 35 c.; 16mo, paper, 15 c.

LATEST WORKS.

NEW TESTAMENT HEROES.

John the Baptist.
12mo, cloth, $1.00.

The second volume of New Testament characters includes the following: John the Baptist; The First Ministry of the Baptist; Baptism unto Repentance; The King's Courts; Art Thou He? None Greater than John the Baptist, yet....; The Manifestation of the Messiah, etc., etc.

"A fascinating study of one of the New Testament heroes. It is neither biography nor sermon, but a happy blending of both."
—*N. Y. Observer.*

Paul: A Servant of Jesus Christ.
12mo, cloth, $1.00.

"Mr. Meyer holds in his hand the key to his reader's heart and conscience. He speaks to conscience with a kind of authority which it is not easy to analyze and yet harder to resist. In this volume he follows Paul's life through in a series of topics, every one of which is rich in food for the Christian life."—*The Independent.*

OLD TESTAMENT HEROES.

Zechariah: The Prophet of Hope.
12mo, cloth, $1.00.

"Mr. Meyer is never more delightful than when he is interpreting the scriptures of the Old Testament. He throws a tenderness into them, and a depth of meaning that the casual reader cannot see. We need this searchlight on some of the old prophecies. We are sure that after reading it, the reader will have an acquaintance with this prophet and his message that he never had before.... The visions of the prophet are beautifully interpreted.... We can recommend this book most heartily to the thoughtful Bible student."—*Christian Observer.*

Saved and Kept.
Counsels to Young Believers. Long 16mo, cloth, 50c.

"It contains twenty-three short addresses, earnest, direct and spiritual, as everything that comes from the pen of this devoted preacher. He writes the preface on his fiftieth birthday, and as he reviews the past, he longs to utilize the lessons and warnings of his life for the benefit of his younger brothers and sisters on each side of the Atlantic."—*The Evangelist.*

Cheer for Life's Pilgrimage.
Long 16mo, cloth, 50c.

"This little book is one of the author's cheery helps for the pilgrim in his life's journey. Like sweet songs his words soothe and comfort and strengthen the heart, and help it to go forward, whether in the peaceful home, or among the temptations of the world. Would that Christians had, or could give, more time to such devotional and upbuilding reading."—*The Christian Observer.*

LATEST WORKS.

Lovers Alway. A Wedding Souvenir.

Marginal Decorations. With finely engraved Marriage Certificate. 16mo, handsomely decorated cloth, nicely boxed, 75c.

"Wise and helpful suggestions in a little book intended to be a memorial of the wedding ceremony and to promote the highest happiness of those united. A marriage certificate, to be filled out, is in place of a frontispiece. In a neat box."—*The Congregationalist.*

Mr. Meyer's Masterpiece.

Our Daily Homily: Genesis to Revelation.

Five vols., 16mo, cloth, each, 75c. The set, boxed, $3.75.

Through the Bible, Chapter by Chapter.

Vol. I. Genesis to Ruth.
Vol. II. Samuel to Job.
Vol. III. Psalms to Songs of Solomon.
Vol. IV. Isaiah to Malachi.
Vol. V. Matthew to Revelation.

The author has selected from each chapter of the Bible a keynote which epitomizes the thought and teaching of the entire chapter. Upon this basis he has constructed brief homilies, which, in their entirety, constitute an exposition of the most important facts and doctrines of Holy Scripture.

"These Homilies are in general to be reckoned among the best things from their author's pen."—*The Outlook.*

Meet for the Master's Use.

12mo, paper, 15c. Cloth, net, 30c.

"Stirring and inspiring. Begins with discourses calling for self-searching, and for repentance and renunciation of sin, and then proceeds with teachings concerning the Christian life."—*The S. S. Times.*

A Castaway, and Other Addresses.

12mo, paper, 15c.; cloth, net 30c.

"Contains the sermons delivered by Mr. Meyer in New York, Boston, and in part in Philadelphia, during his ten days' visit to this country last winter. They treat of the hindrances to spiritual growth and power, of the evil of the natural heart, so hard to overcome, of the only way of curing this evil by getting Christ into the heart, of the work of Christ and of the Holy Spirit, and of the possibilities of the blessed life to which the writer urgently summons his readers."—*The Sunday School Times.*

Peace, Perfect Peace.

A Portion for the Sorrowing. 18mo, cloth, 25c.

"Though the book is a little one, it carries much more consolation than many larger volumes on the same subject. Mr. Meyer does not remand sorrow to an imaginary realm, but facing it in all its wearisomeness, he shows how faith in Christ enables one to bear it and profit by it."—*The Congregationalist.*

WORKS BY HANNAH WHITALL SMITH

THE CHRISTIAN'S
SECRET OF A
HAPPY LIFE
> No. 02. Cloth. 75c.
> No. 03. Cloth, gilt edges. $1.00
> No. 04. White cloth, boxed. $1.25
> Popular edition. 12mo, cloth. 50 cents.

THE HANDY CLASSIC
EDITION. 16mo.
> No. 3. Cloth, gilt edges. 85 cents.
> No. 3½. Decorated white vellum, gilt edges. $1.00.
> No. 4. French morocco seal. $1.50.
> No. 12. Best German calf, embossed. $2.25.
> No. 14. Best German calf, padded. $2.50.
> Nos. 4, 12 and 14 are gilt edges, round corners, boxed.

SWEDISH EDITION.
> 12mo, cloth. 75 cents,

DANISH-NORWEGIAN.
> 12mo, cloth. 75 cents.

GERMAN EDITION.
> 12mo, cloth. 75 cents.

H. W. S. LIBRARY.
> 5 Volumes. 12mo, cloth. $4.50.

Comprising

THE CHRISTIAN'S SECRET OF A HAPPY LIFE.

THE OPEN SECRET.

EVERY-DAY RELIGION.

OLD TESTAMENT TYPES AND TEACHING.

FRANK: THE RECORD OF A HAPPY LIFE.

CHILD CULTURE;

OR, THE SCIENCE OF MOTHERHOOD

> 16mo, decorated boards. 30 cents.

ENVELOPE SERIES OF TRACTS,

> CHAPTERS FROM "THE CHRISTIAN'S SECRET OF A HAPPY LIFE."
> Net, per dozen, 20 cents.

ImTheStory.com

Personalized Classic Books in many genre's

Unique gift for kids, partners, friends, colleagues

Customize:

- Character Names
- Upload your own front/back cover images (optional)
- Inscribe a personal message/dedication on the inside page (optional)

Customize many titles Including
- Alice in Wonderland
- Romeo and Juliet
- The Wizard of Oz
- A Christmas Carol
- Dracula
- Dr. Jekyll & Mr. Hyde
- And more...

Emily's Adventures in Wonderland

Ryan & Julia

CPSIA information can be obtained
at www.ICGtesting.com
Printed in the USA
BVHW04s0228040418
512436BV00019B/256/P